11-6-

£10.00

D1393713

a flower
for every day

a flower for every day

a practical and
inspirational guide to
year-round colour
in the garden

Nigel Colborn

Quadrille

page 1: Foxgloves herald the summer, tempting bees with their speckled throats.

page 2: One of Africa's most elegant wild flowers, *Dierama pulcherrimum* or Angel's fishing rod.

pages 4-5: Needing warm sunshine for its flowers to develop, wisteria blossoms appear in mid to late spring.

First published in 1996 by

Quadrille Publishing Limited

9 Irving Street, London WC2H 7AT

Art editor: Françoise Dietrich

Project editor: Jackie Matthews

Design assistant: Sara-Jane Glyn

Editorial assistant: Katherine Seely

Picture research: Nadine Bazar

Illustrations by Charlotte Wess

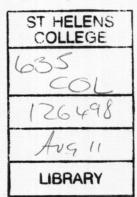
British Library Cataloguing-in-Publication Data

A catalogue record for this book is available from the British Library.

ISBN 1 899988 06 8

Printed in Italy.

contents

Lathyrus vernus '*Alboroseus*'

Introduction

*~ to discover a fresh flower
every day of the year is one of the
greatest joys a gardener can have*

With such an enormous choice of plants in cultivation these days, it should be possible for gardeners everywhere – with a little skill and planning – to pick a different flower every day of the year. Even in midwinter, it should be possible to venture into the garden daily and pick a bloom to bring indoors. Where an exceptionally harsh climate does forbid this, a selection can still be made from flowers growing under glass, in a conservatory or even on a windowsill, so that the constant supply is uninterrupted from one season to the next.

The ever-widening choice of plants means that flowers from the world over can be grown almost anywhere. The tradition of breeding and selecting, in search of bigger and better blooms, has snowballed, with modern hybridizers vying to make their own plants superior. As a result, new species and varieties are being introduced every year; and every year someone thinks of a new way in which to use them.

Every single flower has its own characteristics which make it special and different: the velvet texture of a newly sprung rose, the waxy sophistication of an orchid, the simple beauty of a forget-me-not or the sweet fragrance of a hedgerow violet. With such endless diversity of colour, shape, size and fragrance it is no wonder that flowers have been inspiring mankind since civilization began. And what could be better than to grow a garden full of plants that will allow you to admire a different fresh new bloom every day of the year.

Some of the earliest daisies to flower, Doronicum *or Leopard's bane brightens the spring display with its golden blooms.*

a flower each day...

When it comes to making each day's flower selection, what are the criteria? Colour is important, obviously. In addition, other constituents combine to give a plant its character. Shape and texture have to be considered since it is the unique combination of these which gives a plant its special persona. The soft, half waxy, quartered orange-peel texture of *Clematis orientalis* or of *Kirengeshoma palmata* blooms, for example, is what gives those plants their character. With blue gentians or cornflowers, intensity of colour is the main consideration, although not the only one: cornflowers are cheerful, because they grow in full sun and have waisted, bulging seed capsules, which probably appeal because their outline has something in common with the human form. For all their smallness of stature, Chinese gentians are unequivocal about their superiority, looking inscrutable and regal with their blue throats and regency-striped outsides. No wonder Reginald Farrer, the British plant hunter and alpinist, stood 'rapt in contemplation' before *Gentiana farreri*, the species that was to acquire his name. In his book, *Rainbow Bridge,* he described his find as being of 'so luminous and intense a light azure that one blossom of it will blaze out at you from among the grass on the other side of the valley'. Although it is probably idle to anthropomorphize, one final and more earthy example of plants with special character are the pansies. They are so human, with their comical, scowling faces, that you can almost hear them chatting among themselves.

There are also unlooked-for flowers to be enjoyed. Grasses, even those grown mainly for their foliage, often

LEFT: *Whatever the garden style and however large or small it may be, snowdrops are perfect winter bulbs.*

produce enchanting inflorescences. Hazel nuts (*Corylus avellana*) have showy male catkins, but it was the female flowers, small ruby tufts growing lower down on the twigs, which provided D.H. Lawrence with plenty of brooding symbolism for his novel *Women in Love*. Conifers are less apparent as flowering trees. The pink female flowers on larch are ravishing among the fresh emerald of the emerging needles. On such firs as *Abies koreana*, the female flowers are purple before they transform into cones, and are beautiful, especially when seen in contrast with the deep green, silver-backed needles.

Turning the celebration into reality

Managing to achieve a garden that yields a supply of flowers day in day out can be something of a tall order. Fortunately, rather than advanced gardening skill, all it needs is planning and forethought.

Judicious planting is everything. The most effective way to organize your garden so that perennial interest is maintained, is to assess every plant you grow, as well as every plant on your list of wants, in terms of what it will contribute during its main season of display as well as at other times of year. And, if you assess every square metre of your land, rather than merely each border or bed, in terms of how it will look in winter, spring, summer and autumn, you will soon identify strengths and deficiencies in your planting. To help choose beautiful flowers that are appropriate to your own garden environment, this book discusses more than 500 plants. Depending on where you garden, you will need to select carefully and perhaps even experiment to see just what interesting flowers you can grow.

Enriching a deficient area often consists of no more than adding a plant or two, perhaps just a single one. For instance, a shrub border that looks dull in autumn can be brought to life simply by pleaching the late-blooming but herbaceous *Clematis* x *jouiniana* through one of the duller shrubs or by interplanting with late-flowering lilies. The ground beneath evergreen trees, which is often difficult because so little grows in such dense, dry shade, could be transformed by spring bulbs even if these have to be replaced every two years because the low light levels prevent them from multiplying naturally. The new bulbs you plant will have built up adequate food supplies where they were grown previously to get them through at least one season in a difficult environment.

In the right conditions, certain species can provide a flower on almost any day through the year. The Mediterranean shrub *Coronilla valentina*, for example, is seldom without flower winter or summer, and, if frost free, argyranthemums (marguerites) will bloom endlessly. Such plants are precious, but they are exceptions. Although they might get you out of a spot during flowerless months, your garden will be far more productive if you plan month by month.

As an example of how such planning can work, here is a description of a hypothetical border, planted to provide, if not actually a flower for every day, at least a show of interest right through the year. In a cold region where winters are wet and frost is never far away but where the ground is not continuously frozen, winter is the most difficult time, so we can begin with the darkest weeks.

With careful selection of species, snowdrops can be made to bloom in succession over three to four months, while winter-flowering witch hazel or wintersweet, perhaps with winter jasmine on the wall behind, will be enough to get you through the worst period. As soon as the days begin to lengthen, a run of crocus can begin with *Crocus ancyrensis* and continue over several species until the first epimediums and anemones flower briefly then step aside, metaphorically, for mid-spring flowers like spring peas and honesty.

Then come such early perennials as poppies and lupins followed by a rose selected for repeat flowering and also to harmonize in colour with the perennials. High summer is blessed with penstemons, lavender, perennial mallows and bellflowers, with annuals and tender plants such as nicotiana and *Nemesia caerulea* to plug any gaps and link the display through to early autumn. Perennial asters, dendranthemas (chrysanthemums) and colchicums will ensure continuity of flower until the first of the winter shrubs, probably *Viburnum farreri*, begins to show colour. This, perhaps with a late *Schizostylis* or an early *Iris unguicularis*, will complete the run, closing the circle and ensuring that through the year the garden will present a flower for every day.

9

about this book...

This book is a celebration of flowers, illustrating how their exquisite colour, shape and fragrance can be enjoyed through the year. Starting with the shortest day, it describes the changing seasons week by week, cataloguing the best flowers that can be expected to be in bloom. Clearly, there are weeks when colour and fragrance are scarcer outdoors than at the height of the growing season, but even in the depths of winter there is a small but choice cadre of species to be enjoyed.

It has not been possible to place every plant so that it precisely coincides with its normal blooming period for every region. Because latitude, position in the landmass and ocean currents have such a profound effect on climate, and on how the seasons are scheduled, it is almost impossible to generalize. Even within a single region there is huge variation of flowering dates year by year, especially in winter and spring, because of variations in night temperatures, wind and rainfall.

In addition to describing the flowers, the text includes suggestions for plant associations with consideration given to colour and texture. It also advises on the practical aspects of raising the plants so that they give of their best and produce the maximum number of flowers. Unless stated otherwise, it can be presumed that plants do best in full sun on well-drained soil. Different garden environments are taken into account, and suggestions are offered for plants suitable for growing under glass in cold climates, as well as those that can be cut and brought indoors where the heat will hurry their buds open. Many of the plants described as conservatory or greenhouse subjects will be perfectly happy outside in warm temperate, or tropical regions.

To identify plants recommended for a particular season and to locate them in the text, every plant described is listed alphabetically (under its Latin name) in a special seasonal index of plant names (see pages 140–142); this is followed by a general index.

RIGHT: *Most members of the onion tribe have drumstick flowers in spring and early summer;*

this one is Allium aflatunense.

ABOVE: *Individual cherry trees are lovely enough, especially in full bloom, but how much*

more beautiful to be able to admire a whole grove of them.

Clear skies and warming winds herald the new season. The sun rises earlier each day and stays with us a little longer, giving more light to entice winter-weary plants into new growth

Spring

Spring climates are fickle, with sudden squally winds and cold snaps, yet nature sees to it that, on average, the weather improves each day. Flowers come and go in dramatic succession, their colours clean and bright, their fragrance sweet or spicy to tempt early bees. Emerging with petals folded against cold mornings, they open wide in midday sun. Even though spring vegetation lacks the luxuriance of the summer display, forays into the garden will always be rewarded, even on the coldest, earliest days. There is always something new to delight in. Snow-white cherry blossom, for example, is never so lovely as when set against the pewter of stormy clouds. Buds swell rapidly. Daffodils appear like vertical spears, then angle their opening blooms at the still low sun as the weather warms.

RIGHT: *Fickle weather brings plenty of surprises, but these snakeshead fritillaries are not set back by a scattering of untimely snow.*

FAR RIGHT: *Anemone nemorosa 'Allenii' is one of an interesting number of selected forms of the wild European wood anemone.*

Every spring flower is an event. Even young leaves can resemble flowers, especially when the sun shines through them, turning their hue to translucent gold

Spring promise

Spring is the most restless of seasons, when each day's weather comes as a surprise. Sharp night frosts are often redeemed the next day by glorious sunshine. Winds can be devastating, but they blast away the last of winter and often prelude warm rain, which, with sunshine, gently heats the soil, enticing the plant world from its winter dormancy.

As the season advances, colour creeps into the landscape. The browns and duns of winter give way to a green that is so intense in lawn and pasture as to be almost fluorescent. At first, colour is dotted sparingly about the garden – a single camellia bloom here, an early primrose there. As spring sunshine coaxes more and more flowers, however, soon there are clusters and then solid drifts of colour.

Plants which grow from bulbs, worthwhile at any time of the year, reach a crescendo in spring. Woodland species such as bluebells bloom and set seed in the few weeks of warm sunlight before emerging foliage on the trees above throws them into relative darkness. Bulbous plants from dry regions such as the Mediterranean or southern Africa cram their entire life cycle between winter chill and summer drought, briefly popping up in profusion in the arid landscape. Such canny evolutionary developments pay dividends to gardeners who can crowd their beds and borders with a glorious mix of bulbs, which have the kindness to disappear after their spring bonanza making room for the summer display that follows. Besides such staples as daffodils, tulips and crocuses, there are peacock-blue scillas and irises and anemones in both pastel and vivid primary shades. While the lower-growing fritillaries are sometimes mysterious in their sombre shades of brown, purple and green, the huge crown imperials are downright sinister, betraying their presence with a distinctive foxy odour and carrying clusters of hanging, veined flowers which weep a constant dew of tears.

The garden's shape and texture changes during spring as winter's hard profile, dominated by skeletal trees and man-made structures, softens into the less clearly defined outlines of developing vegetation. Herbaceous plants begin to expand, bringing more rounded contours to borders. Shrubs and trees clothe their hard silhouettes in a mantle of foliage and flower. Even evergreens, whose leathery leaves have survived the coldest weather, alter in texture and colour as their buds break to produce brighter, softer young foliage.

New landmarks appear daily, notching up the season's progress. The first bee feeding on primroses, for instance, or the appearance of furry catkins surprises and delights you. Later, you notice that the air is teeming with flying insects or the temperature is warm enough to go outdoors without bothering to put on a cardigan or jacket. Climbing plants come into bloom, starting with the earliest clematis species but soon joined by spring honeysuckle. Rose foliage, at first liverish or brick-coloured, turns green as it develops then, all of a sudden, the first fragrant summer rose opens, and spring is behind you.

15

LEFT: Tulipa *'Fantasy' has feathered swirls of colour.* ABOVE: Rhododendron occidentale, *is a fragrant deciduous species (see page 37).* ABOVE RIGHT: *A selection of border auriculas.*

Early spring is the time of year when the first and choicest of the smaller rhododendrons are at their best. Deciduous species such as the yellow azalea *Rhododendron luteum* need a run of warm weather to coax open their flowers, but when they do bloom, their fragrance is so heady that a single shrub can perfume a shaded dell for metres around. It is not long before the whole tribe of rhododendrons and azaleas will be a riot of colour. (Rhododendrons and azaleas are discussed in more detail on page 37.)

Epimediums, herbaceous members of the *Berberis* family, make natural companions for a planting of azaleas and rhododendrons, gracing the ground at their feet and providing extra colour. An early blooming species that has especial charm is the ground-covering *E. x youngianum*. Even though it is more dwarf than most, flowering at about 15cm (6in), it does not hide its blooms beneath the previous year's foliage, a habit that can spoil the effect of some members of the genus. The common form is a beautiful lilac mauve, while the cultivar 'Niveum' has pure white flowers which show up more effectively in the shady situations that the plant prefers.

The butter-bright yellow of lesser celandines (*Ranunculus ficaria*) are a cheery sight along the hedgerows and in the wild-flower gardens of colder climes. Their cousin the Asian buttercup (*R. asiaticus*) grows well outdoors in warm regions, but is best raised under glass where winter temperatures drop below freezing, grown either as a pot plant or for cutting for floral arrangements. In the wild, there are both vivid yellow and startling red forms. The red of the petals is of such an intensity, though, that it is almost difficult to look at in strong sunlight. Glorious in their natural state, Asian buttercups are also one of the oldest species to have attracted the attention of early European breeders who began their transformation into the cultivated forms so familiar today. Under glass they can be grown in any compost.

LEFT: *Among highly bred seed strains of* Ranunculus asiaticus, *'Accolade' is grown for its compact habit and the rounded rose shape of its double flowers.*

ANEMONE FULGENS and *EUPHORBIA MYRSINITES*

These two Mediterranean beauties make perfect companions for a well-drained site in full sun. The vivid yellow-green blooms of fleshy, grey-leaved *Euphorbia myrsinites* go handsomely with red or scarlet flowers, especially those of *Anemone fulgens*. In hot sun, the anemones will begin to open at the start of spring, producing a succession of bright 5-8cm (2-3in) blooms. These are excellent for cutting, especially if they are brought indoors while still in bud so that they can open in the warmth of a room.

SAXIFRAGA MOSCHATA 'Elf'

Many of the mossy saxifrages develop into soft, evergreen mounds which provide subdued decoration throughout the year. Such species as *Saxifraga moschata* have been used to develop garden hybrids of great beauty. Some, for example 'Cloth of Gold', have coloured foliage, but 'Elf' is at its best in spring when its star-shaped, carmine-pink flowers appear on short, wiry stalks. Although some of the mossy saxifrages grow scruffy with age, 'Elf' retains its neat, compact shape. Protect it from the midday sun and rejuvenate it periodically by taking small rooted sections from an old plant and replanting them.

RANUNCULUS FICARIA 'Brazen Hussy'

Bright as buttons, lesser celandines stud hedgerow bases from the beginning of spring. The sheen on their golden petals is as shiny as patent leather. Regarded by some as a weed, celandines are welcome in the gardens of the more liberal minded, at least as such approved cultivars as the double-flowered 'Lemon Queen', the rich orange 'Cupreus' or the deep bronze-, almost black-leaved 'Brazen Hussy'. Celandines do best in moist soil and enjoy sun or dappled shade.

DORONICUM ORIENTALE 'Magnificum'

Looking more like summer blooms than early spring ones, the bright yellow daisy flowers of leopard's-bane, which are carried on stems up to 45cm (18in) tall, are good for cutting. The vivid green, heart-shaped foliage makes a lovely foil for other spring flowers as well its own golden blooms. The most dependable species is *D. orientale* (syn. *D. caucasium*), of which 'Magnificum' is an improved form. For tiny gardens, the dwarf and fully double cultivar 'Frühlingspracht' (syn. 'Spring Beauty') is an excellent choice. Doronicums prefer rich moist soil that does not bake in summer. Beware of vine weevils.

MERTENSIA PULMONARIOIDES

The forget-me-not family (*Boraginaceae*) provides a rich choice of species. Certain genera from the New World, including *Mertensia pulmonariodes* (syn. *M. virginica*), have a special beauty. Although demanding in their requirements, each spring they reward you with glaucous blue-grey foliage and soft azure flowers. Acid or neutral soil

is preferred, in gentle shade and moist conditions. In the Old World, the closely related lungworts are much easier to grow and are valuable for their broad, generously marked foliage as well as for their early flowers.

FORSYTHIA

Perhaps the best known symbol of early spring, the cheerful flowers of the shrub forsythia bloom on naked winter stems. The most commonly grown cultivars are not necessarily the best. *F. x intermedia* 'Lynwood' certainly has the most vividly coloured flowers, but the climbing species *F. suspensa* makes better use of space, being perfect for furnishing a wall or fence. In a container, the tiny shrubs of *F. viridissima* 'Bronxensis' will not exceed 60cm (2ft). Grow in full sun and fertile soil. Prune immediately after flowering to promote new wands for next year's blossom.

Although the predominant flower colour of spring is yellow, few plants are more closely associated with the early season than forget-me-nots. Plant breeders have worked harder with *Myosotis alpestris* than with any other species of their large family (*Boraginaceae*) to produce dozens of good garden forms. There are several named cultivars, including some with pink or white flowers. None is as pleasing as the bright blue, however. The first flowers open while the plants are still compact and rounded, nestling like gems among the slightly coarse foliage. As the plants mature, they open out, gaining height and width to create a misty drift of blue, which makes a soft, indeterminate background for the more solid colours of tulips, in almost any shape or size. Or the plants can be naturalized among shrubs or woodland to create a floating haze of colour among stems and trees.

Like many other members of the family *Boraginaceae*, forget-me-nots are woodland margin plants, which enjoy shelter from the strongest sunshine yet dislike dense shade. If the plants are left to die back naturally in summer after flowering, they will self-sow in most borders. Before clearing away the plants, shake them to release all the seed.

Other early flowering members of the forget-me-not family include the genus *Omphalodes*, so called because their flowers resemble a navel (*omphalos* is Greek for navel). One of the prettiest is *O. cappadocica* which grows wild in Turkey. Its brilliant sky-blue flowers are set off by dark, metallic-grey foliage. Although chance seedlings do appear, this is a well-mannered plant which will bloom year after year without needing any special treatment other than gentle shade and a soil that contains leafy material. An even easier plant, but one inclined to be invasive, is *O. verna*. Its flowers are also a clean sky blue, but its foliage is less handsome. Its habit is to creep, forming thick mats, which, in gentle shade, prove to be relatively weed proof in summer.

ABOVE: *Forget-me-nots, such as* Myosotis alpestris *'Royal Blue', are as useful for*

naturalizing in grass or a woodland garden as for siting in a formal garden border.

Tulips that have been forced for blooming indoors will be over their best by now, but outside the first of the species will begin to appear. In bedding schemes, for example, their broad, glossy foliage makes a handsome foil for the first tufts of blue flower from the forget-me-nots. Later, when the tulips have achieved their full height and come into bloom, the accompanying forget-me-nots will have evolved into a 'mist of blue. Early flowering and hardy enough to shrug off whatever the weather might throw at it, the brilliant scarlet, multi-headed *Tulipa praestans* is small enough to use in a rock garden but showy enough for a border or to be used in a container. Grown near the contrasting flowers of, say, Spanish gorse (*Genista hispanica*) or among doronicums (see page 18), the effect is dramatic, although not especially long lasting.

The first member of the *Rosaceae* family to flower, long before the roses themselves bloom in summer, is a geum. In moist, alkaline soil, the water avens (*Geum rivale*) begins to throw out reddish stems topped with drooping or nodding flowers in pale, rather dusky pink. Good garden forms include the bright, coppery pink 'Leonard's Variety', a cultivar that copes with drier soil than its bog-loving wild cousins and flowers valiantly well into summer.

With weather still chilly, the greenhouse and conservatory continue to have their attractions. Most of the autumn and winter blooms – cyclamen, cinerarias and ornamental *Solanum* – are approaching the end of their season, and as summer flowers have yet to come, this is a period when foliage plants are important. Developing new foliage as soon as the days begin to lengthen, the genus *Begonia*, comes to the rescue. Shrubby begonias such as *B. coccinea* and *B. scharffii* (syn. *B. haageana*) also start to produce flowers to complement their handsome leaves. Damaged or leggy plants should be trimmed fairly hard back to encourage new shoots. Leafy begonias, such as *B. rex*, can be divided and repotted.

LEFT: *Hybrid primrose series such as* Primula *'Leda' have little in common with their wild forebears, whose honest yellow blooms mark the beginning of spring.*

TULIPA 'Olympic Flame'

Fancy hybrid tulips bloom outdoors from mid-spring onwards. They can be brought into bloom early by being forced under glass. After flowering, tulips can be lifted and either replanted in a resting ground or dried off so that plant nutrients in the foliage can return to the bulb where they are stored. Store dry bulbs in a cool but frost-free place, and plant them out as soon as is convenient in the autumn.

PRIMULA AURICULA 'Janie Hill'

Intensive breeding and selection of *Primula auricula* began in the late eighteenth century, when hobbyist florists became obsessed by the idea of developing the fragrant flowers to ever greater beauty and perfection. Cultivars robust enough for garden use vary through a wide range of generally subdued colours from pale beige to deep maroon or purple black. In sun or partial shade good companions include *Omphalodes verna* (see page 18) and the low-growing, vivid golden-green *Euphorbia polychroma*. Show auriculas, grown in containers in a cool greenhouse, may have less vigour than border kinds, but their exquisite form makes them worthwhile. Flowers carry a dusting of green or have blooms picked out in bands of three different shades, making them look like eighteenth-century jewellery. Auriculas need free-draining, gritty soil and to be kept quite dry during winter.

FRITILLARIA IMPERIALIS

Crown imperials are hardy bulbs that have been in cultivation since ancient times. The species has orange flowers on dark stems up to 1m (3ft) high. The leaves are arranged round the bottom two thirds of the stem with an extra tuft of foliage on the stem tip, held above the flowers like a topknot. Cultivars include the yellow form 'Lutea' and the huge red-flowered 'Rubra Maxima', whose intense blooms have dark veining in the petals. Inside the flower, the dark base surrounds a white eye that looks like mother of pearl and weeps a clear nectar which collects like a teardrop. For those who enjoy such freaks, there is a form with variegated foliage known as *F. imperialis* 'Aureomarginata'.

21

Perhaps the charm of the daffodil rests in its cheerful colour and the briefness of its appearance

Narcissus

Extensive collecting and careful breeding over the centuries has given rise to a bewildering number of cultivated daffodils and narcissi, ranging from minuscule pot subjects such as *Narcissus asturiensis*, which barely reaches 8cm (3in), to such huge, coarse hybrids as 'King Alfred' or the double-flowered 'Golden Ducat'.

Development among large-cupped narcissi has transcended various colour barriers. There are dozens of varieties with pink trumpets, such as 'Passionale', and so-called reverse bi-colours, with outer petals darker than the trumpets. One of the earlier, and still excellent, reverse bi-colours is 'Spellbinder', a flower with pale mustard petals and a trumpet suffused with pale lemon. White large-cup cultivars such as 'Mount Hood' and 'Cantatrice', which begin the palest waxy lemon but soon achieve milky purity, look ravishing in large drifts.

Of the later-flowering narcissi, few can surpass the beauty of the poet's narcissus (*N. poeticus*), which grows wild in northern and central European meadows. The true poet's narcissus or pheasant's-eye (*N. poeticus recurvus*) is one of the last to flower. The petals of its flat blooms bend back slightly, and its tiny yellow cup is red-rimmed like a bird's eye. The unmistakable fragrance is unique, even when it blends with flowering lilacs and the first of the mock oranges.

Originating mostly from south-western Europe, the genus *Narcissus* is generally less tolerant of dry conditions than are most other spring bulbs. Yet in the wild, such tiny species as the hoop petticoat daffodil (*N. bulbocodium*) are to be found growing in the damp meadows of the foothills of the Pyreneean mountains. When grown in gardens, these are never happier than when seeding around in moist soil or in the short turf of a simulated Alpine meadow.

After flowering, narcissus foliage should be left strictly alone and allowed to die down naturally. Feeding is unnecessary, as is dead-heading, exept for the sake of neatness. As bulbs become overcrowded, they shoud be divided and replanted.

BELOW: *Among the first daffodils to flower are* N. pseudonarcissus, *the wild kind which inspired the English poet William Wordsworth.*

BELOW: *The true poet's narcissus (*N. poeticus recurvus*) grows profusely in the upland meadows of central Europe.*

ABOVE: *Sweetly scented, with bottle-green foliage and tiny-cupped, yellow blooms, the true jonquils (*N. jonquilla minor*) flower late.*

RIGHT: *Of all the narcissus hybrids, the* Cyclamineus *group, with their narrow, swept-back pointed petals, are among the most appealing of the genus. Many, like this 'Little Witch', are early flowering.*

ABOVE: *An American dog's tooth violet (*Erythronium revolutum*) makes a colourful woodland carpet in early spring. The deep pink flowers have gracefully reflexed petals.*

Although days are growing warmer, leaves have yet to emerge on the trees, leaving woodland floors still bathed in sunlight. All over the temperate world, deciduous woodland carries a rich flora of quick-blooming species which take advantage of the few weeks of full daylight before the trees come into leaf, shading the ground so densely that growth becomes almost impossible. In Europe, wood anemones (*Anemone nemorosa*), primroses (*Primula vulgaris*), oxlips (*P. elatior*) and bluebells (*Hyacinthoides non-scripta*) are abundant. North-eastern American woodlands sport drifts of *Trillium grandiflorum* (see right below), whose pure white flowers turn pink with age, and false spikenard (*Smilacina racemosa*), which has feathery sprays of white flowers. In Asia, dense, blue spikes and ferny foliage of *Corydalis flexuosa* appear under the trees, followed later in the season by the gorgeous blue poppy flowers of the tall *Meconopsis grandis* or *M. betonicifolia*.

Several spring-flowering genera have woodland species in more than one continent. These can be planted together as long as they enjoy similar habitats. They will thrive and look attractive together. Thus, the European dog's tooth violet (*Erythronium dens-canis*) can associate harmoniously with the North American pink-flowered *E. revolutum* (see left). In some cases, their colours and flower shapes are similar, but other erythroniums could add golden, cream or sharp yellow blooms, all turning up their petals as daintily as *E. revolutum*.

Erythroniums are at ease in the company of epimediums (see page 17), and will also complement such general favourites as jonquils or daffodils, lungwort (*Pulmonaria saccharata*), its blue-and-pink flowers set off so well by the stippled, evergreen foliage, and the dicentras. One of the best garden forms is *Dicentra formosa* 'Stuart Boothman', which has coppery pink flowers and a pewter-grey cast to its ferny foliage. Long after flowering, lungworts and dicentras continue to carpet the ground with decorative leaves.

LATHYRUS VERNUS 'Alboroseus'

The spring pea begins to flower before it is fully grown. By mid-spring when it is fully grown at just over 30cm (12in), it is covered with blooms and buds, which continue to open until the beginning of summer. The pea flowers of the common species are a warm, rich magenta. Beautiful alternative forms include pale pink 'Alboroseus' and a breathtaking, blue-flowered subspecies, *L. vernus cyaneus*. Spring peas harmonize well with other pink to purple spring perennials, including aubrieta and *Lunaria rediviva*, the pale mauve perennial honesty.

CHIONODOXA FORBESII

Known as glory of the snow because they come up so early, the majority of chionodoxas are blue. Mid-blue *C. forbesii* (syn. *C. lucilae*) is available in a white form, 'Alba', and two pink, 'Rosea' and 'Pink Giant'. The smaller-flowered *C. sardensis* is darker blue. Chionodoxas go well beneath yellow-flowered shrubs such as *Piptanthus laburnifolius* (see page 33). They seed freely and can colonize large areas quickly. Free-draining soil in sun or partial shade is best for chionodoxas. They thrive in the poorest of soils.

TRILLIUM GRANDIFLORUM

There are many species of trillium, but none is quite so ravishing as wake-robin, one of the most conspicuous North American woodland flowers, whose pure white blooms turn pink as they age. Trilliums prefer leafy, acid or neutral soil in dappled shade. Once established they need little attention other than a mulch of leaf mould.

CAMELLIA 'Inspiration'

In the woodlands of Japan and Korea, evergreen wild camellias bloom beneath the shelter of taller trees, but for our gardens there are hundreds of different hybrids to choose from. In a frost-free region or in a conservatory, we can indulge ourselves with *C. reticulata*, the most sumptuous of species, whose white and multi-coloured blooms sometimes reach almost 15cm (6in) across. The hybrid *C.* 'Inspiration' has smaller leaves, making the flowers look even larger. Although it is frost hardy, *C. japonica* and its hybrids are more reliable outdoors in colder gardens. Camellias need acid or neutral soil. Tolerant of full sun, they do best in dappled shade.

DAPHNE TANGUTICA

On alkaline soil some of the daphnes can make delightful substitutes for dwarf rhododendrons. Evergreen and compact, *Daphne tangutica* is an ideal choice. It is blessed with a spring crop of purple-pink buds which open in mid-spring to sweetly scented, white-flushed blooms. Good companions are *Omphalodes cappadocica* (see page 18), with large, vivid blue flowers and pleasing grey foliage, and

Dicentra formosa 'Stuart Boothman' (see page 25), which has bronze to grey filigree foliage and wine-pink blooms. Other evergreen daphnes include the small *D. collina*, which has scented purple-pink flowers, and the spurge laurel (*D. laureola*), whose green flowers are intensely fragrant. Daphnes are not long lived and benefit from being grown in a sheltered site on free-draining soil which does not dry out too much in summer.

FRITILLARIA PERSICA

Among the taller-growing fritillaries, *F. persica* must be one of the most sombre coloured. The 1.5m (5ft) spikes of brownish-purple flowers have a distinctive matt texture which contrasts strongly with the glaucous grey foliage. This curious-looking sun-loving plant needs fertile soil. In shaded, leafy, acid soil, the liverish tones of the darker trilliums, such as *T. sessile* and *T. rubrum*, produce similar results.

With the staggering number of varieties available, cherry blossom typifies the spring scene, in both garden and woodland. In addition, many other members of the genus *Prunus*, including plums, almonds, apricots and even laurels, contribute their attractive spring blossom. From Japan, for instance, comes the modestly beautiful Japanese apricot (*P. mume*) (see page 126) whose blooms arrive so early.

Japan has given us a rich supply of dozens of ornamental cherries, such as *P.* 'Tai-Haku', whose huge white blossoms precede the foliage. Extra special among Japanese cherries are the extraordinary greenish-flowered *P.* 'Ukon' and the relatively late-blooming *P.* 'Shirofugen', whose buds are mid-pink but whose very double, pale pink blossoms harmonize with the reddishness of the emerging foliage and often persist until the tree is in full leaf. The cultivar 'Shirotae' has a wide, spreading habit so that in old trees the horizontal branches benefit from props. On a fine day, they are a delight to sit under in contemplation of the blue sky above through the mass of white blossoms.

Among smaller members of the genus, *P. tenella*, which seldom reaches more than 1m (3ft) in height, has a quieter charm. The variety *P. tenella* 'Fire Hill' has single, rich pink flowers. To keep the plant tidy, it can be pruned to ground level immediately after flowering and thus makes as good a mixed-border subject as a plant for the shrub garden.

Evergreen members of the genus are known as cherry laurels. Although the common species *P. laurocerasus* is good for little other than hedges or windbreaks, there are cultivars of immense charm, especially when in bloom. Of these, the dwarf *P. laurocerasus* 'Otto Luyken' has the prettiest leaves — narrow, pointed and pricked like ears along the stem — and showy white flowers held in tight, upright spikes.

Tree species of *Prunus* tend to be short lived, most surviving less than 40 years, and so are best left unpruned to avoid the possibility of infection of their wounds by disease.

Underplanting a cherry, or if you are lucky enough to have room for them a group of cherries, can present both challenge and opportunity. White narcissus, for example, grown in grass beneath the spreading branches makes a fine continuation of the colour scheme, and on lengthening spring evenings they give a ghostly effect. With pink-flowered cherries, lemon-coloured narcissus, such as the variety 'Ice Follies', could make a richer combination, as could the deep blue flowers of scillas and chionodoxas (see page 25).

27

Pink in bud, the fragrant blossom of Prunus *'Shirofugen' opens white then pink.*

Naturalizing flowers in grass, whether under trees or in the open, is a gardening technique which deserves wider and more imaginative use. Although spring bulbs are probably the plants most frequently grown in turf, a surprising number of broad-leaved species, including primulas, wild cranesbill (*Geranium*), scabious and those handsome relatives of the buttercup, the globeflower (*Trollius*) all lend themselves to grass culture.

Mid-spring often sees a marked contrast between gentle maritime climates, where some plants will have been in flower for months, and more extreme continental weather systems, where suddenly increasing temperatures cause everything in the garden to catch up fast. Besides such bulbs as grape hyacinths (*Muscari*), crocuses and *Scilla peruviana*, which seem to pop up from nowhere overnight, other plants are also re-emerging from the ground. Small, but distinctive, *Corydalis flexuosa* first appears with divided, bronze-tinged foliage, soon followed by kingfisher-blue flowers. Also blue is Russian comfrey (*Symphytum caucasicum*). The coarse, rough leaves of this great, sprawling perennial are inclined to be messy in summer, but in spring the penetrating mid-blue of its tubular flowers makes it a fine subject for a wild garden.

In moist meadows, pale lavender cuckoo flowers, or lady's smocks, are appearing. The double form, *Cardamine pratensis* 'Flore Pleno', makes a charming, long-lasting display for cottage gardens. Cuckoo flowers are easily increased by planting torn fragments. Other double-flowered favourites for cottage gardens are the perennial wallflowers, particularly the golden, shrubby variety *Erysimum cheiri* 'Harpur Crewe'. Double the petals means double the fragrance, but these fussy plants are short lived unless replaced at least every second year with young cuttings taken in late spring.

As spring progresses, the taller perennials begin to flower, columbines often providing the vanguard. The European species, *Aquilegia vulgaris* (see page 35) and its mountain relative *A. alpina*, have generated a range of medium- and short-spurred flowers in blue, white, pink and purple shades. Long-spurred North American species in red, orange and yellow have given rise to some magnificent hybrids, but such true species as red *A. formosa*, yellow-and-red *A. canadensis* and yellow *A. longissima* (see left), are much lovelier. The many different aquilegia species make a long flowering season.

LEFT: *The flowers of* Aquilegia longissima, *one of many columbine species from North America, have extra-long spurs, which give them a unique grace.*

SMYRNIUM PERFOLIATUM

Biennials, particularly those which have distinctive characteristics in their formative period, make a very special contribution. *Smyrnium perfoliatum*, a 60cm-1m (2-3ft) member of the carrot family, has attractively divided foliage in its first growing season. In its second year it shifts from a background role to being a star performer when, in a surprisingly short time in mid- to late spring, a flower spike erupts from the rosette of basal foliage to produce bracts and flowers of an incredibly luminescent yellow green. Beware, though. This plant self-seeds with a vengeance and will soon carpet an entire area unless unwanted seedlings are pulled up and discarded.

MUSCARI PALLENS

Grape hyacinths (*Muscari*) grow wild in arid Mediterranean regions, where springs are cool and moist but summers are very hot and dry, baking the bulbs and thus ripening them to ensure good flowers for the following year. *Muscari pallens* is a distinctive species with plump, bead-like flowers in bright blue, each with a pale rim. In free-draining soil and full light, grape hyacinths will seed around. Disturbing the soil around the parent bulbs will distribute the small bulblets which form around them.

PRIMULA VERIS

For many people, the cowslip symbolizes the arrival of spring. The flowers are sweetly, although faintly, fragrant and last well in water after being cut. It is one of Shakespeare's most frequently mentioned wild flowers, and when the fairy in *A Midsummer Night's Dream* says that she must: 'go and hang a pearl in every cowslip's ear,' she is referring to the tiny pearl-like stigmas that can be found at the centre of some flowers.

Although they are natural grassland plants, cowslips thrive equally well in good border soil. Without competition from grass, they grow up to 25cm (10in) high and have larger flower heads, making them suitable for picking for indoor use. This is worth doing for their scent alone as it is subtler yet sweeter than that of freesias. Cowslips are best raised from seed.

RIBES SPECIOSUM

Among several plants sent to Europe in 1824 by a young Scottish plant hunter, David Douglas, exploring north-west North America, was the flowering currant (*Ribes sanguineum*). It grows in almost any conditions, and covers itself each spring with showy pink blossoms. From further south in the same continent, an even more handsome currant is *R. speciosum*. Like a gooseberry bush with pretensions, this shrub has shiny foliage and dark, bristling stems hung each spring with long, graceful red blooms.

ORNITHOGALUM NUTANS

Common bulbous plants of the Mediterranean region, stars of Bethlehem (*Ornithogalum*) grow in scrubland. The hanging, grey-green striped blooms of *O. nutans* give it the common name of drooping star of Bethlehem. Although they are stimulated into growth by winter rain, these plants need a hot, dry summer to ripen the bulbs to ensure good flowers the following year. In a cold region, the bulbs need to be planted in the sunniest spot. In heavy soil, a handful of sharp grit placed beneath each bulb will assist drainage and prevent the bulb from rotting.

VIOLA LABRADORICA

Part of the charm of the scentless *Viola labradorica* lies in the dark hue of its foliage, which makes a pleasing contrast with the pale purple flowers. It makes a fine companion for wood anemones and primroses, since the darkness of the foliage sets off their flowers so well. It is a good-natured plant which can survive harsh conditions and can grow in either dense shade or full sun. But be warned. This plants seeds around freely, soon developing thriving colonies which could invade large areas unless unwanted seedlings are pulled up and discarded.

At the height of spring, as the green mantle of growing plants continues to cover the ground, the flowers of lily of the valley (*Convallaria majalis*) are sometimes hidden by foliage. But, that sweet, penetrating scent is hard to miss. Indoors, a picked bunch of the white, waxy, rounded bell flowers can fill a room, or even a whole house, with fragrance. Lily of the valley will colonize the shaded area under a tree or below flowering shrubs such as *Viburnum x carlcephalum*, itself a pretty good plant for fragrance. Given space, it can be used as a fairly invasive ground cover, and it is useful for shady places that tend to dry up in summer. The plants can sulk for a season or two after planting before growth takes off.

On the woodland edges and shady banks, following on from primroses (see page 135), the sun-loving cowslips (see page 29) reach their flowering climax. They are most at home with lady's smock (*Cardamine pratensis*) (see page 29), white-flowered star of Bethlehem species such as *Ornithogalum nutans* (see left, centre) or *O. umbellatum* and humble wild daisies (*Bellis perennis*). In the wild, cowslips are sometimes found growing with terrestrial orchids, especially *Orchis morio*. When naturalized in a meadow, they seldom exceed 15cm (6in), but in the rich soil of a garden border they will grow double-sized flower heads on long stems.

Out in the sunshine, *Thermopsis montana* makes a wonderful foil for red tulips, especially the old-fashioned blood-red variety 'Couleur Cardinal'. They form shapely spikes of butter-yellow flowers which contrast pleasingly with the very dark three-lobed leaves. They can be troublesome spreaders, but such large, showy flowers so early in the year, even in cold soil, are worth any trouble the plant may cause.

The sight of a mature apple tree in full bloom is one of spring's highlights. Carmine in the bud, apple flowers open to look like pale pink, single roses, each with five petals and a central tuft of pale gold stamens. Bees love them.

ABOVE: *Lily of the valley (*Convallaria majalis*) enjoys a cool root run, preferably not too dry*

in summer. It flowers profusely in sites where there is little direct sunshine for part of the day.

One of the first roses to flower, and therefore susceptible to chilly winds or late frost, is the yellow Banksian rose (*Rosa banksiae* 'Lutea') (see opposite). This vigorous, double-flowered climbing cultivar had been grown in Chinese gardens for centuries before it was introduced to Britain, via India, by the rosarian J.D. Parks in around 1824. The button blooms lack scent, but their soft primrose colour goes perfectly with Chinese wisteria (*W. sinensis*) if the two plants are allowed to grow into each other on a warm, sheltered wall.

Chinese wisteria is the earliest wisteria to bloom. It is soon followed by the Japanese species *W. japonica*, which is available in a wider range of colours, including purplish pink 'Rosea', white 'Alba' and a dark, double-flowered form known as 'Kokkuryu' (syn.'Black Dragon'). The stronger and coarser, white-flowered silky wisteria (*W. venusta*) is also a magnificent climber.

Wisteria can sometimes be shy to flower, especially in areas where rainfall is high or light levels are low. For the best results, they need to be planted in sharply draining soil in a warm position. All wisterias flower better when hot sun has ripened their stems during the preceding season. If training them on a wall, be sure to select a surface that receives plenty of direct sunlight. An interesting alternative to using wisterias as wall plants is to grow them in containers, pruning and training them to form small, gnarled, weeping trees. Pruning is essential to encourage flowering and to keep the plants to the desired shape. In late summer, take all the long, wispy leads out, cutting back to around three or four buds from the point where the thin

Caltha palustris is one of the earliest-flowering and prettiest of the marshland plants.

32

growth joins the main stem. This resulting stump will mature into a fruiting spur which produces flower buds. Some experts recommend a second pruning in late winter, but I have found my wisterias flower profusely enough after a single late summer cut.

After its long winter dormancy, pond life is beginning to stir, and water plants start to come into growth. Cold and forbidding though the water may be, this is the correct season for renovating pond plantings. Such bog plants as the lovely yellow king cups (*Caltha palustris*) will be in bloom already, but irises, sedges and other marginal species can be taken out of their planting baskets and carefully divided before replanting. Fishing out water lily roots is a colder, dirtier job. Planting the lilies in aquatic baskets equipped with loops to enable them to be hooked out of the water does make the task a little easier. Without these there is no alternative but to wade in and to grope for the big, fleshy rhizomes.

Once they are in hand, cut off sections, making sure that each piece carries its complement of small buds and baby leaves. The best planting method is to line a lily basket with hessian (burlap) or synthetic fibre netting then to pack this with special aquatic compost. Alternatively, you can use a mix of garden soil, grit and such organic material as peat or rotted leafmould. Plant the lilies firmly then spread a thick layer of coarse gravel over the surface of the compost to discourage fish from rooting about in the compost.

Pretty alternatives to water lilies with surface-floating leaves that are so important for shading water include water hawthorn (*Aponogeton distachyos*), an African plant with sweet-smelling flowers and odd-looking edible fruits. The leaves go dormant in midsummer, but emerge again before autumn. The fringed water lily (*Nymphoides peltata*) is not a water lily at all, yet it has shapely yellow blooms, each with a slightly ruffled edge, and floating rounded leaves.

SYRINGA VULGARIS 'Madame Abel Chantenay'

Lilacs have been symbols of spring romance for generations. Today, there is a varied repertoire of varieties available to gardeners, and, as much of the earlier development took place in France, many have French-sounding names. Good common lilac cultivars include the double-flowered, reddish-purple 'Charles Joly', the pinkish 'Belle de Nancy' and the creamy white 'Madame Lemoine' and 'Madame Abel Chantenay'. In addition to the common lilac, there are other beautiful species, notably S. reflexa, whose flower panicles hang gracefully, rather like those of the later-flowering buddlejas. All lilacs flower best in full sun.

PIPTANTHUS LABURNIFOLIUS

Deep bottle-green stems, which hold their colour all winter, make this unusual shrub distinctive in all seasons. In mild areas it is evergreen, holding old foliage until the new leaves emerge with the flower buds in spring. The buds themselves are clothed in silvery fur, making a contrast with the dark colour of the scale leaves. These soon split to reveal bright yellow pea flowers produced in tight bunches. The three-lobed leaves are reminiscent of laburnum foliage, but are darker and more shapely. The plant is often cut back to the ground by severe frost, but should regenerate from the roots.

ROSA BANKSIAE 'Lutea'

The first rose to flower comes from China. Named after the great eighteenth-century British botanist, Joseph Banks, Rosa banksiae is a thornless climber whose faintly scented flowers emerge in clusters at the very beginning of the growing season. They are produced in such profusion that the drama of a mature plant in full fig is considerable. The form 'Lutea' is the hardiest of the group. Its double flowers are golden at first but turn primrose as they open and mature. The plant makes a pretty companion for the blue-flowered Wisteria sinensis, which blooms at roughly the same time and enjoys the same conditions, that is a sunny site in free-draining soil.

33

In the woodland garden, gorgeous blue Himalayan poppies (*Meconopsis*) begin to usher in the end of spring. Several species have flowers with such an electric glow they have to be seen in the flesh to be believed. Easiest to grow is *M. betonicifolia* (see left), the species introduced to Western gardens in the 1950s by the last of the great plant hunters, Frank Kingdon Ward. Good seed strains will produce long-lasting perennials with kingfisher-blue flowers. For strength of colour and size of flower, however, the queen of this group has to be *M.* x *sheldonii* 'Branklyn', whose huge, nodding blooms are as blue as a peacock's neck. Grown in shelter and gentle shade, in cool, leafy soil, Himalayan poppies will tolerate a certain amount of lime. As they are not especially long lived they need to be propagated regularly to maintain stocks. Sow seeds in autumn to expose them to frost, or sow in pans in spring, having first refrigerated the seeds to stratify them and initiate germination.

Tulips will soon be over, but cottage varieties such as the pink *Tulipa* 'Clara Butt', named after the great contralto of the earlier part of this century, provide a late display. These are useful for introducing a little colour among the summer-flowering perennials which, although full of promise, are hardly interesting at this time of year.

By now, the first of the mock oranges (*Philadelphus*) are opening their strongly scented blooms. The double snow-white flowers of the cultivar 'Virginal' last well, but those of 'Beauclerk', which are creamy white with cerise or purple centres, have a stronger fragrance. For the back of the shrubbery, the Midland hawthorn (*Crataegus laevigata*) carries white blooms which later become red fruits that will be enjoyed by birds in the autumn. Other, more ornamental forms of hawthorn include the double rose-red 'Paul's Scarlet'. Unfortunately, as its compound flowers do not fruit this form is less wildlife friendly.

LEFT: *Exquisite blue Himalayan poppies (*Meconopsis betonicifolia*) have become popular garden plants during the last half century.*

ZANTEDESCHIA AETHIOPICA

Despite its Ethiopian-sounding name, the white arum lily is also a native of southern Africa, where it grows in profusion along road-side ditches and riversides as well as in every moist field. The term 'lily' applied to this plant is a misnomer, although the flowers are identical in colour to the Madonna lily (*Lilium candidum*). Zantedeschias are marshland plants, preferring wet ground that is frost free.

AQUILEGIA VULGARIS 'Adelaide Addison'

Columbine, the common name for *Aquilegia vulgaris*, means 'dove' or 'pigeon formed', and is so named because the flower resembles five pigeons arranged on a round perch. Although some of the characteristics have been lost in garden varieties, the basic shape is still recognizable. Among desirable garden forms, bi-coloured 'Adelaide Addison' is one of the most distinctive. Its white-centred, Oxford-blue flowers are comprised of densely packed petals, but still retain the classic columbine shape. Other interesting cultivars include double pink 'Nora Barlow' and white 'Nivea' (syn. 'Munstead White'). Columbines grow and seed freely in amost any soil, prefering dappled shade or sun. Old plants flower less well than young ones, so be prepared to re-sow every few years.

IRIS 'Knick Knack'

Dwarf bearded irises, of which *Iris* 'Knick Knack' is just one of dozens of examples, are not only coloured in glorious hues such as blues, yellows, maroons, browns and beiges, they exhibit utterly the last word in tasteful colour combinations. *I.* 'Gingerbread Man', for example, is tan with a contrasting sky-blue beard, whereas *I.* 'Blue Pools' combines bright azure with pure white, like puffy clouds on a clear sky. Dwarf bearded irises enjoy sharply drained soil in full sun. To guarantee free flowering divide the rhizomes regularly.

35

You do not need a country estate to enjoy the staggering

range of medium and dwarf rhododendrons and azaleas

Rhododendrons

FROM THE TOP:

Rhododendron occidentale has fragrant pale pink or white blooms with yellow throat markings. The foliage turns russet in autumn.

Flowers of R. 'Naomi' contrast with the softer pink of R. yunnanense and R. 'Golden Spur' in this composite of blooms.

R. 'Hino-giri', a compact, neat-growing evergreen azalea, is smothered every spring in wine-coloured blooms.

Because of their size, and their relatively short flowering period, the larger rhododendron species and hybrids have tended to be confined to the grander gardens of the larger landowners. Large-flowered Loderi hybrids such as 'Pink Diamond' or the cream-coloured 'Julie', the huge, flop-leaved *R. macabeanum* with its clusters of purple-blotched, yellow bell-like blooms, and the tall, red-flowered *R. arboreum* are all at home in large woodland gardens.

Among rhododendrons suitable for smaller gardens, those raised from *R. yakushimanum* are popular. The species itself is prettier than any of its children, however. It has a neat, compact habit with young leaves covered with a silvery bloom. More mature leaves are glossy dark green with beautiful rust-coloured backs. The dark pink buds open into funnel-shaped blush flowers which gradually fade to white before the petals fall. This plant is tough and, unlike the majority of its cousins, thrives in full light in the open. Hybrids include 'Torch', 'Snow Maiden' and 'Koichiro Wada', but if you have room for one only, choose the true species.

Azaleas, many of them deciduous, are also available in small or medium sizes and, in certain varieties, have the added advantage of powerful, heady fragrance. Some of their colours are very strong. In the yellow, salmon and orange range, they need careful placing if they are not to clash with the softer pinks of other rhododendrons. Among the best for fragrance are the Ghent hybrids. These grow relatively large, up to 2m (6ft), and have honeysuckle-shaped blooms. Smaller and more compact are the Rustica hybrids whose sweet-scented blooms are double. Cultivars include the salmon 'Freya' and the redder 'Norma'.

Being shallow rooted, rhododendrons and azaleas are not suited to drought or hot, dry positions. They will not tolerate lime and, though some species survive in neutral soil, most prefer it to be acid. They are happiest in woodland conditions, so in gardens they respond to generous mulching to retain soil moisture.

LEFT: *One of the larger rhododendrons, evergreen R. 'Seven Stars' grows up to 3m (10ft) in height. It is covered with two-tone pink flowers from mid- to late spring.*

CLEMATIS 'Helsingborg'

The choice of spring-flowering clematis available to gardeners has increased dramatically in recent years, not only among such Asian species as C. macropetala and C. montana, but also among that beautiful European species, C. alpina. One of these recent additions is C. 'Helsingborg', which is outstanding for the richness of its flower colour. The sepals, which in clematis resemble petals, are a rich royal blue, but, unlike other varieties of C. alpina, the insides of the flowers are a dark purple blue. Pruning is not necessary with C. alpina, but if the plant grows too large or becomes untidy, it can be pruned after the main flower flush in late spring. To ensure a good crop of early flowers, feed clematis during summer and ensure that their roots are kept moist and cool, either by mulching or by growing plants around their bases.

38

STRELITZIA REGINAE

Southern Africa has given the world a rich heritage of invaluable garden flowers, from such florist's favourites as gerberas and chincherinchees to such garden indispensables as nemesia, diascia and osteospermum. Among bulbs and tubers, we have the Cape to thank for agapanthus, nerines and many gladiolus species. But for uniqueness of form, the genus *Strelitzia* takes the prize. For indoor or outdoor use, the bird of  paradise flower (S. reginae), with its pointed 'bill' and orange wing-like petals, is remarkable. The plant was first collected by the British during the reign of George lll (1738-1820), and was named after his wife, Queen Charlotte of Mecklenburg-Strelitz. It is not frost hardy, and, although excellent in a conservatory, young plants may be reluctant to flower for several years. They should be fed with a potash-rich fertilizer.

As spring moves into its final weeks, gardeners are busy preparing for the summer display to come in later months. This is a time of feverish activity, especially in cold climates where tender plants that needed protection from frost must be hardened off now before being planted out. Pots and urns are stripped of bulbs, primroses, wallflowers and winter pansies which saw service through the early part of the season ready to be replanted with container-loads of petunias, lobelias, pot geraniums, fuchsias and other half-hardy flowers in readiness for the next season.

On walls, fences, arches and pergolas, climbing plants move up a couple of gears in the race to cover their supports, softening hard lines and preparing to provide months of colour, fragrance and interest. Among early climbers, the spring-flowering clematis offer so much for so little effort. The three species that provide most of the colour are C. montana, C. alpina and C. macropetala.

C. montana, the Chinese mountain species, is inclined to be a thug, strangling and engulfing whatever comes within its grasp. Where space is not limited, however, and a good cover is wanted, this is the plant to choose. Several pink and white forms are available. Perhaps the most dramatic form is the subspecies C. montana sericea, sometimes sold as C. spooneri. The white flowers, which open to almost 8cm (3in) across, are so abundant in spring that their petals touch, creating a dazzling avalanche of blossom.

More restrained in habit and even more beautiful, C. alpina, the European mountain species, is perfect for pergolas or for weaving through other wall plants. In the wild, the nodding, four-sepalled flowers are a rather dusky blue, but among cultivars, clean colours include the pale blue 'Columbine', the deeper blue, large-flowered 'Frances Rivis', 'Burford White' and the dark purple-blue 'Helsingborg' (see left, top). Similar in habit to C. alpina. C. macropetala sports masses of double flowers which have a more tufty appearance. Both species have fluffy, silvery seed heads.

Clematis hybrids that flower before the longest day of the year usually have the largest blooms of all. Varieties such as pale blue 'HF Young', white 'Marie Boisselot' and the double 'Countess of Lovelace' should not be pruned until after they have flowered, if at all. Subsequent blooms produced later in the season will not be so large, and in the case of double varieties usually appear as single flowers.

In full sun, the rich purple tones of *Allium aflatunense* (see right, top) preview the blowsy purples to come later in summer. This plant needs companion plants at its feet to hide the foliage, which begins to brown and die before the buds have fully opened. Echoing the purple, but in a gentler, cleaner mauve, *Chamaecytisus purpureus* is a spring-flowering broom whose foliage makes a pleasant, green ground cover long after the blooms have failed.

At this stage in spring, many of the earliest blooms will have already faded and some plants, notably spring bulbs, will be dying down prior to turning dormant. Resist the temptation to cut back their foliage until it has completely died and turned brown and crisp. Leaving the plants intact will ensure that all nutrients have sufficient time to be returned to the bulbs where they are stored until growth begins again the following year.

Dying daffodils in particular can be unsightly, but it is better for the plants to let them die back naturally than to knot or fold the foliage. If you dislike the ugliness of their aftermath, plant them among later-flowering perennials so that they will grow up to hide the dying bulb foliage.

Tulips do not take offence to being lifted immediately after flowering, provided they are replanted intact or are laid out somewhere cool but dry to allow their tops to die back and their bulbs to mature.

ALLIUM AFLATUNENSE

Ornamental garlics have immense garden value. Many flower between spring and summer, some with considerable architectural benefit in a general planting. *Allium aflatunense*, with its straight stems and tight, spherical umbels of tiny, star-shaped flowers in rich purple, makes a fine display. *A. christophii* is also useful, not only for the silvery purple flower globes in spring, but also for the dried seed heads in autumn (see page 80). *A. karataviense* has broad, deeply creased foliage which is a dark blue-green with purple undertones. An open, sunny position in well-drained soil is essential.

PULSATILLA VULGARIS

At the end of spring, the pasque flower produces silky seed heads that are almost as pretty as the flowers themselves. As the seeds ripen, each with its individual feathery parachute, they become lighter and are lifted from the stem to be borne away by the wind. To save seed to sow, it must be collected by hand as soon

as it will pull off easily, before the wind carries it away. It can be sown in any seed-sowing compost, in a warm place. Young plants should emerge within a few weeks.

GERANIUM SYLVATICUM

Wood cranesbill is a common European wild flower which has become a popular border plant. The flowering period comes early, towards the end of spring, but unlike many of the cranesbills, this one does not repeat flower. Cranesbills, the name is derived from the bird's beak shape of the seed heads, belong to the same family as pot geraniums (more correctly pelargoniums) and the storksbills. They prefer dappled shade, but will grow in any soil.

ABOVE: *The transatlantic crossing of two wild species of Solomon's seal has resulted in*

Polygonatum x hybridum, *a variety with unbeatable hybrid vigour.*

At the end of spring, mixed herbaceous plantings are reaching their first crescendo as hardy geraniums, or cranesbills, such as the pale pink *Geranium lancastriense* or the taller, pink *G. endressii*, begin their summer-long succession of flowers. In mild regions, the startling pink blooms of the outsize *G. maderense*, a native of the island of Madeira, will have been on show for weeks, perhaps in company with its impressive compatriot, *Echium nervosum*.

The first phloxes begin to open, not the tall perennial kinds, but alpine species such as *Phlox stolonifera*, whose cultivars include the delightful creamy white 'Ariane', and the startling blue *P. divaricata* 'Chattahoochee'. These small phloxes perform best if divided up on a regular basis.

Solomon's seal (*Polygonatum*) is a genus that spans the Atlantic, occurring wild in North America, Europe and Asia. Most of the species used in gardens share the characteristics of tall, angled stems with paired leaves and flowers hanging either singly or in clusters. In autumn, many of them produce red berries. The garden form *P. x hybridum* (see left), a cross between *P. multiflorum* and *P. odoratum*, has tubular, green-tipped white flowers. There are double and variegated forms, but both lack the vigour and charm of the straightforward cross. Solomon's seal is wonderful for planting among ferns in dense shade.

A natural companion for Solomon's seal is *Smilacina racemosa*, which it resembles closely until creamy tufts of flowers appear on the ends of the stems. Its smaller, creeping relative, *S. stellata*, is neither spectacular nor particularly well behaved, spreading invasively in shade, but it has pretty star-shaped flowers. Woodland cardamines (fomerly dentarias) make attractive companions, too. Not only the mauve-flowered *Cardamine pentaphyllos* but also the creamy *C. enneaphyllos*. These are short lived in flower, but have attractive ground-covering foliage.

ANEMONE SYLVESTRIS

A plant that provides a double display has double the value, especially in a small garden. The snowdrop anemone, or windflower, produces its clean white flowers, which are centred with tufts of golden stamens, from mid- to late spring. In late summer and autumn, another distinctive effect is created when the seed heads begin to erupt, appearing like white cotton bolls. Another bonus is that in partially shaded conditions, flowers will pop up throughout the growing season. The root stock of this carpeting plant spreads best, but not invasively, in light, sandy soils. Allow to self-seed.

DIGITALIS PURPUREA

Foxgloves, so-called because their flowers make finger stalls for fairy folk, combine so much talent and beauty that most gardeners, especially if they have more shade than they would like, would not be without them. The seed series 'Excelsior' is said to be an improvement on the wild form, partly because the flowers are arranged all the way around the tall stem rather than down one side. One of the charming features of the wild foxglove, however, is its tendency to hang its blooms on one side of the stem towards the sun. Since they produce thousands of seedlings, it is easy to select foxgloves to improve the strain. Allow colonies to develop then pull out those which do not conform to what you require. If selecting for white or pale forms, pull out seedlings with dark stems before they flower. Thin plants to a minimum of 45cm (18in) apart to ensure maximum flowering size.

CISTUS x CYPRIUS

The first of the rock roses heralds the end of spring. In the heat of the day, the aroma of the evergreen *Cistus* x *cyprius* (syn. *C. ladanifer*) is distinctly balsamic, and the leaves are sticky. Labdanum (not to be confused with laudanum), a perfumed resin, is extracted from this plant. To perform well, rock roses prefer hard, dry conditions, baking in hot summer sunshine, their roots in poor, stony soil. If over fed or grown too lush, they will succumb more easily to winter frost and rain.

PAEONIA SUFFRUTICOSA 'Alice Palmer'

Paeonies combine the simple charms of a classic flower shape, grand size and sumptuous colour. Species bloom from mid-spring, when the primrose-coloured *Paeonia mlokosewitschii* and red *P. officinalis* are at their best, until midsummer, when the last of the *P. lactiflora* hybrids make their display. Extra special species include the small herbaceous *P. cambessedesii*, which has flowers the hue of crushed strawberries, and *P. suffruticosa*, a tree paeony which has given rise to many cultivars, including 'Alice Palmer'. The flowers of 'Rock's Form', now alas almost unobtainable, are like white crushed silk with deep purple centres. Some herbaceous paeonies prefer fertile soil which does not dry too much in summer; tree paonies are susceptible to late frost and consequently should not be planted in a hollow frost pocket.

DIGITALIS x MERTONENSIS

The colour of crushed strawberries, *Digitalis* x *mertonensis* is a hybrid of two species, the common foxglove (*D. purpurea*) (see page 41) and *D. grandiflora* (syn. *D. ambigua*). The flowers of the former are rosy purple with deep speckling in the throat. The latter, a beautiful garden plant in its own right, has creamy blooms with rusty marks in the throat. The vigorous hybrid has deeper green leaves than the common foxglove and shapely flower spikes which sometimes exceed 1m (3ft). This short-lived perennial needs to be replaced with new seedlings at least every other year.

SYMPHYTUM GRANDIFLORUM

Most people enjoy a love-hate relationship with the comfreys. Love for the endless succession of nectar-bearing tubular flowers, produced from intriguingly whorled stems which uncurl like fiddleheads. Hate because the plants can be horribly invasive. *Symphytum grandiflorum* will cover a large area with frightening speed, but its creamy flowers are so pretty and irresistible to bees. It makes a good ground cover for a shady spot on poor soil.

Positively the last of the tulips at the end of spring, *Tulipa sprengeri* produces small but dazzling scarlet flowers above emerald foliage. A wild species from Asia Minor, it behaves more like an herbaceous perennial than a bulb, seeding and spreading quite freely, although it takes several years before seedlings reach flowering size. Dappled shade is preferred, but do arrange for the plants to receive direct sunlight for at least part of the day: the sight of the flowers glowing in slanting sunlight is one of the finest, and also one of the last, experiences of the garden in spring.

Bold groups of big oriental poppies add excitement to a well-tempered border. In addition to the scarlet of *Papaver orientale*, there are many interesting shades among its cultivars: the deeper, more intense red of 'Beauty of Livermere'; gentle shades of pink as in 'Mrs Perry'; the lilac-pink of 'Cedric Morris'; 'Lavender Girl', which is much darker than lavender, rather like the colour of stewed damsons with a drop of cream stirred in; and 'Blue Moon', whose huge papery blooms are not blue at all but pale lavender-pink, and whose petals are crinkled.

Shrub and tree collections will soon be running down after their display of blossom. Already, the flowers of such garden favourites as *Laburnum* x *watereri* 'Vossii' are falling. The horse chestnut trees (*Aesculus*) have replaced their white, candle-like blooms with embryonic conker fruits, although some chestnut species and buckeyes, such as *A. indica* and *A. parviflora*, will continue to flower for some weeks yet.

So spring completes the transformation from bright but hesitant beginnings, with crocus and other blooms counted first singly and then by the dozen, to the burgeoning riot of vegetation that leads into the summer climax. As the longest day of the year approaches, we can look back on spring, remembering the more joyful displays. And we can look forward to the floral banquet that summer has in store for us.

RIGHT: *Each double bloom of* Papaver rhoeas *Shirley Series makes a fleeting appearance before its petals fall, but the flowering period lasts for many weeks.*

ABOVE: *Striking opium poppies (*Papaver somniferum*), spikes of* Salvia sclaria turkestanica

and abundant roses reach their flowering peak at summer's end.

What luxuriance in the summer garden!

What vivid colours, varied textures and

bewitching fragrances one can find!

With each passing week comes

a succession of

glorious displays

Summer

Flowers are at their brightest during the long, warm days of the summer season, and foliage, still young enough to look fresh and clean as it approaches the climax of its growth, provides cooling contrasts to their brilliance. Each flower brings its own special character into the garden, whether boldly stated or set quietly in the background. Together, they create a symphony of delight that runs through change after change as the season advances. And because no other season offers so rich a palette, the summer garden presents endless possibilities for delightful contrasts and harmonies. The primary colours – red, yellow and blue – can be used for drama in bedding schemes, while on a gentler note flowers in pastel shades can be harmonized with grey or silver foliage.

45

RIGHT: *Happy in sun or semi-shade,* Bellis perennis *is available in a number of prettily coloured shades and variously sized double flower heads.*

FAR RIGHT: *Highly fragrant, the double deep pink flowers of the climbing* Rosa *'Rosy Mantle' show up well against the dark green foliage.*

The rose is the very essence of summer: rich perfume, warm colours, fullness of flower and a bountiful supply of gorgeous blooms all summer long

Summer abundance

Different perfumes enrich the warm summer air. In the rose garden especially, there is a heady cocktail of scent: the sugary undertones of Damask roses, the richer, fruitier tang of the rugosas and the clean, delicate scent of the old Tea roses. If you look at rose petals closely,

you will see other differences, not only in colour, but also in texture, shape and size, from the small ruffled petals of the low-growing burnet roses to the gently puckered cabbage blooms of the old-fashioned hybrids. Blending with these in any well-planned garden come the flatter, satin-textured blooms of clematis, whose garlands can be trained among the rose branches. The bee-like blue flowers of delphinium make a cooler contrast. Even among the structural planting, compact lavender hedges are purple with blooms, attracting bees and butterflies.

Summer is the best time to experiment with contrasts and harmonies. In bedding schemes, massed boldly coloured blooms merge to create a single surface of brilliant hues or weave an intricate pattern. Pastel colours, dianthus, perhaps, or pale cranesbills, can be grown among grey or silver foliage. Strident red poppies can be coaxed into

softer focus by being framed with misty sprays of white Queen Anne's lace (*Anthriscus*) or made more dramatic by being teamed with peacock-blue cornflowers or vivid orange marigolds (*Calendula*).

A succession of special specimen flowers helps to heighten interest at any chosen spot. Containers are useful in this respect, perhaps brought to the garden's seating area as their occupants come into bloom, a rare paeony for early summer, perhaps, and fragrant lilies for the warmest days. And, whatever the climate, summer is the time for tropical blooms – a potted hibiscus, for instance, or the glorious royal-blue flowers of *Tibouchina urvilleana* (syn. *T. semidecandra*).

When the light fades at the end of each day and coolness comes as

sweet evening relief, paler colours take over, glowing in the twilight. Flowers that looked washed out in sunshine become dominant in the evening border, appearing almost magnified, while their vivid daytime neighbours shrink and disappear. Night fragrance, too, differs from day, since night-blooming flowers attract different pollinating insects, and the perfume hangs heavier on the still air. Jasmine is so strong as to be almost intoxicating, nicotiana is sweeter. In cooler climates, little can beat the alluring, lemony tang of the honeysuckle *Lonicera periclymenum*.

The choice of flowers for cutting is never better than in high summer, but many are likely to wilt unless handled with care. Very early morning is the best time for gathering bouquets, preferably before the dew has vanished. Plunge the cut stems immediately into deep buckets of water and leave the flowers in a cool place before arranging.

'Summer's lease' may have 'all too short a date', as Shakespeare mused in his famous sonnet, but with plants maturing, blooming and fading in such rapid succession, there is no time to regret their passing.

LEFT: *Massed blooms provide a glorious and varied summer display.*

ABOVE: *Lavender cut ready for use.* ABOVE RIGHT: *Time to relax in the summer garden.*

DEUTZIA x ELEGANTISSIMA 'Rosealind'

You could be forgiven for mistaking this deciduous deutzia shrub for the other main member of its family, the mock orange (Philadelphus). The two genera share the same lax habit and suckering growth, and when the deutzia flower buds open, the pink or white cup-shaped flowers are like miniature versions of mock orange blossom, but with five petals rather than four and produced in small, uncrowded sprays. One of the most elegant forms is the cultivar 'Rosealind', which has shell-pink buds and flowers. Deutzias thrive in either sun or partial shade, on well drained, fertile soil. They need pruning to keep them young and compact. Remove branches that have flowered to make room for new growths which will bloom the following season; the best time to do this is immediately after flowering to allow the new stems maximum time to mature.

LUPINUS 'The Chatelaine'

Lupins were introduced to Europe from North America in the early nineteenth century. Before they suffered a serious decline due to virus disease, Russel lupins were once the height of fashion. Today, a comprehensive range produces flower spikes of the original magnificent quality in reds, creams, blues, pinks and a selection of good positive bi-colours. 'The Chatelaine', for example, bears 1m (3ft) spikes of pink-and-white flowers.

CENTAUREA 'Pulchra Major'

This perennial cornflower is fascinating, not so much for its handsome silver-grey foliage or the soft magenta-pink of its flowers, but rather for the extraordinary papery calyces. One cannot resist touching them and listening to the rustle as they are stroked, or marvelling at how light from a setting sun seems to shine right through them. A valuable addition to the border, it contributes long-lasting character and beauty. Culture is easy: full light and reasonable soil that is well drained but not too dry.

When the first roadside poppies bloom, there is no mistaking that summer is truly here. The field poppy (*Papaver rhoeas*), with faintly crinkled, scarlet petals, each with a black blotch at the base, has been developed into the pale pink poppies known as Shirley Series (see page 42) and a strain called Angel's Choir, which has charming colours and ruffled petals. A single packet of seed suffices for the first sowing of these free-seeders. Provided they have sun, field poppies will grow just about anywhere.

Red poppies fire up a mixed border in sunny weather, when intense light conditions need ever stronger colours to create impact. Contrasting the red with the vivid blue of annual cornflowers such as *Centaurea cyanus* (see page 52) heightens the effect. At twilight these strong hues disappear, allowing paler shades to take over. With careful planting, the whole effect of a border can be transformed as the subtleties of the palest pastels become more apparent.

For middle-of-the-road colours, the perennial cornflower species, *Centaurea montana*, comes in a more sombre blue than the annuals, although there are white and pink forms too, and its close relative, *C. dealbata*, is a rich cerise. Both plants respond well to being cut back mid-season, providing a second display later. A number of summer-flowering perennials, such as cranesbills, lupins, penstemons and several of the bell flowers also respond to such drastic treatment, especially if fed and watered immediately after the cutback.

At this time of year, giant herbaceous plants can introduce instant 'architecture'. These grow at an astonishing rate to tower over the border or to rear up at the side of a pathway. Most exciting is the thistle *Onopordum nervosum*, a branching biennial monster armed with sharp prickles in leaf, stem and flower, but with wonderful soft, silvery grey-green foliage. In good soil, it scales almost 3m (10ft). It is best grown from seed sown in the ground where it is to flower.

ABOVE: *Annual poppy cultivars in pink, lemon, white and even dove grey have been developed from the field poppy* (Papaver rhoeas), *one of the prettiest roadside flowers.*

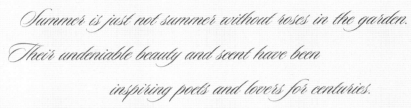

Summer is just not summer without roses in the garden. Their undeniable beauty and scent have been inspiring poets and lovers for centuries.

Roses

No wonder roses are the world's most popular flower. The huge variety and scope of their colour, size and configuration, combined with their often long flowering seasons means that there are roses to suit every taste and planting scheme over the entire summer season and even stretching into autumn.

The Chinese appreciated the special charm of roses early on and were growing them in their gardens thousands of years ago. Unlike European roses, Chinese roses repeat flower. After their introduction into Europe in the eighteenth and nineteenth centuries, they became the basis of almost all the hybrid groups which followed. Among the first of these were the frost-tender Tea roses, such as Rosa 'Maréchal Niel' and 'Lady Hillingdon'. The first of the hardy Hybrid Teas, 'La France', soon followed, from which has proliferated the huge wealth of large-flowered modern hybrid roses, encompassing almost every colour except blue. The acid yellows, salmon shades and sharp, scarlet reds arose from the introduction of genes from other species during the twentieth century. The modern rosebud shape, pointed at its centre with the first petals curling back, is also an oriental characteristic inherited from the original China roses and is quite distinct from the flat-topped, quartered structure of old western varieties.

While modern roses offer an endless variety of colour, it is often at the expense of scent. Early roses tend to have the strongest fragrances. The original wine-red apothecary's rose (*Rosa gallica*), for instance, is sweetly scented. More popular is 'Rosa Mundi', now known as *R. gallica* 'Versicolor', which is striped pale lilac and dark pink. Among the best of the old varieties for fragrance are Damask roses. Some, for example 'Ispahan', grow to around 2m (6ft) and can be used as low climbers. When dried, the pink blooms are almost as fragrant when fresh.

FROM THE TOP:

Rosa gallica 'Versicolor', one of the oldest favourites, has striped mid-season blooms in two tones of pink. They last for about one month.

The cultivar R. 'Graham Thomas' has the rounded flower shape and strong fragrance of old roses, and it repeat flowers.

One of the whitest of modern hybrid roses, R. 'Iceberg' (syn. 'Schneewittchen') is available in both bush and climbing forms.

LEFT: *The crimson buds of fragrant Rosa 'Gros Choux d'Hollande' open to form large, rounded blooms in a clear, luminous pink.*

CENTAUREA CYANUS

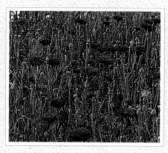

In a cornfield, the annual cornflower's particular shade of dark but brilliant blue contrasts dramatically with the yellow-gold of ripened wheat or barley. Plant breeders have doubled up the petals (technically sterile ray flowers) and selected for a widening range of colours, including pink and white as well as dark muddy purple, bi-colours and picotees. To get closest to this plant's beautiful wild simplicity, grow the single blue or a single-coloured strain like 'Blue Diadem' in association with field poppies (see page 48), marguerite daisies (*Leucanthemum vulgare* or *Argyranthemum frutescens*, especially yellow cultivars like *A.* 'Jamaica Primrose'), or the parchment *Osteospermum* 'Buttermilk'.

DIERAMA PULCHERRIMUM

No plant is so graceful or so unforgettable as the wandflower in full bloom, especially when its arched stems move gently in a breeze. The long flower spikes bow slightly under the weight of the flower buds, which look as though they are made from rice paper. These open into tiny sprays of lilac, mauve or pink conical flowers, which hang from the main stem like small papery bells. If planted to arch over water, wandflowers live up to their other colloquial name, angel's fishing rod. Originating from southern Africa, they relish sandy, free-draining soil that is damp in winter and spring.

ROBINIA HISPIDA

The rose acacia is a beautiful slender tree or shrub whose bright green ferny foliage appears very late in spring and turns sharp yellow before falling in autumn. The bright pink flowers, which resemble wisteria blossom, are produced in large enough numbers to make an attractive display, set off by the foliage. Also of especial garden value are rose-pink *R. kelseyi*, a shrub best grown against a warm wall, and the tougher *R. pseudoacacia*, of which the golden-leaved, white-flowered 'Frisia' is deservedly popular.

Choosing good companion flowers for roses (see pages 51) is almost as important as selecting the roses themselves. Blues go especially well with the pinks and reds of roses, and the tall spires of blue delphiniums contrast pleasingly with the rounded rose shapes. Dependable varieties include pale blue *D.* 'Lord Butler' (see right), at its best now until midsummer, and, later, *D.* x *belladonna* cultivars such as gentian-blue 'Wendy' and the huge 'Pacific' hybrids. Also available in pink, lavender or white, delphiniums are excellent for cutting.

Good for growing with delphiniums, but even taller, is *Crambe cordifolia*. Its coarse, dark foliage belies the beauty of the vast, airy sprays of white flowers which open at the very beginning of summer. In good soil, this plant needs support. The lower-growing, edible seakale (*C. maritima*) has beautiful glaucous, grey foliage and tighter sprays of sweet-smelling, off-white flowers. It will grow in poor soils, even gravel.

Laburnum and wisteria are well over by now, but the pea flowers of false acacias are in bloom. White-flowered *Robinia pseudoacacia* is one of the easiest to grow. One of the prettiest for blossom, however, is the pink-flowered *R.* x *margaretta* 'Pink Cascade' (syn. 'Casque Rouge'). These fairly fast-growing trees are inclined to be brittle in a gale, unless planted in a sheltered site. They flower best if grown in relatively poor soil. A beautiful, but less hardy, species is *R. kelseyii*, whose large pea flowers are a soft, shell pink.

Clematis, particularly the early large-flowered hybrids, are reaching their climax. If they are to be pruned, it should be done immediately after flowering. Left alone, however, such varieties as sky-blue *C.* 'Lasurstern', deeper blue 'The President' and blowsy, lavender-blue 'Mrs Cholmondeley' will re-flower. Clematis like their roots cool in moist, semi-shaded fertile soil, exactly the conditions enjoyed by such terrestrial orchids as *Dactylorhiza fuchsii*, whose handsome purple spires are colouring up now and whose leaves will cool the roots.

RIGHT: *Although fully perennial, delphiniums such as 'Lord Butler' perform best if they are reproduced every year either from cuttings or by division.*

ABOVE: *Flowering from early summer until the end of the growing season, penstemons are among the most useful of herbaceous perennials. They are easy to reproduce from soft cuttings.*

One of the finest contributions the New World has made to our gardens, penstemons, bring so much more than mere summer colour. Varying from tight-growing shrublets such as *Penstemon fruticosus* to tall, stately perennials like the burning red *P. hartwegii*, wild species grow in a variety of habitats from the Canadian Rockies all the way down to Mexico. Breeding and selection have given us a precious set of long-lasting, colourful perennials, well endowed with flower power and available in colours to please even the most discriminating tastes. Of especial note are the green-shaded blue *P.* 'Sour Grapes', the tall lavender 'Alice Hindley', ruby-red 'Garnet' and, among the hardiest of the group, the smaller-flowered, light pink 'Evelyn'. All these plants flower continuously from around the longest day until the first of the frosts. Most of these sun-loving plants respond best to fertile, moisture-retaining soil. Cut back hard in spring to promote flowering.

Behind the penstemons, later-flowering shrubs include the indigoferas, members of the pea family from China. These have bright green, soft, ferny leaves and carry successions of small, bunched pea flowers in pink, cerise or pale purple. Most popular, and probably the best species for garden use, is *Indigofera heterantha*. The mauve flowers appear in racemes (lots of small blooms to a single stem) spaced evenly along the branches and last for weeks on end. Good companion shrubs include the larger, arching *Rubus* 'Benenden' (syn. *R.* 'Tridel'). Its showy white blooms precede those of the indigofera, but the coarse, wrinkled foliage makes a pleasing contrast. Watch out for it swamping its neighbours, though, and prune savagely back if it steps out of line. Both plants are sun lovers.

The tall bearded irises blend happily with both penstemons and indigoferas. They are spectacular although short lived in flower. Divide and replant the rhizomes every second year, soon after they have finished flowering, to be rewarded with top quality blooms produced in abundance.

DIANTHUS 'Sops-in-Wine'

In mediaeval Europe, the flower heads of certain pinks were used as a cheap substitute for cloves to flavour mulled wine, hence the term 'Sops-in-Wine'. Originally, the name was applied to a group of pinks. Today, 'Sops-in-Wine' pinks are maroon with white markings. There are dozens of cultivars with similar markings, including the light crimson-and-white *D.* 'Gingham Gown' and 'Waithman Beauty', whose red-and-white contrast is altogether more sombre. To keep plants young, take cuttings or layer by pegging stems in the soil every second year.

PELARGONIUM 'Splendide'

The genus *Pelargonium* is exclusively African. Most species were introduced to Europe during the eighteenth century, when the plants were dubbed 'geraniums'. Many have aromatic foliage, others are notable for the beauty of their blooms. In the wild, one of the most elegant is *P. tricolor*, a plant that is notoriously tetchy and difficult in cultivation. Happily, the desirable garden form, *P.* 'Splendide', is more amenable if it is grown in sharply draining compost and kept fairly dry.

ARGYRANTHEMUM 'Mary Wootton'

From the warm Atlantic islands of Madeira and the Canaries, members of the daisy family grow into sizeable shrubs, some of them flowering for long periods. Of these, the tender argyranthemums are of inestimable value. In containers or beds, trimmed, topiaried or left entirely to their own devices, they flower copiously and constantly. The commonest form is the white marguerite (*Argyranthemum foeniculaceum*), but the closely related *A. frutescens* provides a more interesting range of colours in yellows, oranges, peach tones and pinks. *A.* 'Mary Wootton', an old favourite, is a double form with well-shaped rays and full centres in soft pink. Argyranthemums grow in any soil, even the poorest, and flower best in full sun. Pinch back regularly to keep the plants in bloom.

GERANIUM PRATENSE 'Mrs Kendall Clark'

Cranesbills have three great strengths: most flower for long periods; their colours are in that valuable zone that connects pink with blue, running through every imaginable shade of mauve, lilac, lavender, glowing purple, shocking pink and white; and most are fully hardy and good-natured about where they are planted. In the wild, the field cranesbill (Geranium pratense) is clear blue with veining visible in the petal, but it has some fascinating garden variations which include white, pink, double and, prettiest of all, 'Mrs Kendall Clark', whose petals are a unique shade of pearly grey-blue with veining.

CAMPANULA LACTIFLORA

From tiny alpines such as Campanula cochleariifolia to the huge, 'cup and saucer' flowers of the biennial Canterbury bells (C. medium), campanulas, or bell flowers, are shaped so precisely like bells that you can practically hear them ringing. Apart from the occasional pink or lavender, the most common colours are shades of blue. Tall and almost shrub like, C. lactiflora has generous sprays of 2.5cm (1in) flowers. Seedlings are variable but one fine selected cultivar, with lavender to pink flowers, is 'Loddon Anna'. C. lactiflora is a long-lived perennial with a large tap-root. Feed annually and divide plants every few years.

IRIS and ASTER

The iris, a short-lived genus, has distinctive flowers. With but three stigmas and stamens sandwiched between upper and lower petals, they are fascinating to examine in isolation. Placing them near the rayed flowers of a member of the daisy family enables comparisons to be made. The aster is a member of the daisy family (Asteraceae), part of a larger group formerly called Compositae because what look like individual flowers are, in fact, colonies of florets (see page 71).

Climbers grow so fast in these long, lazy days that you can almost watch them spreading their cover over wall and trellis. In frost-free areas, plumbago is smothered with thousands of pale blue, primrose-shaped flowers. It can be a space hogger, and under glass it will threaten neighbours unless its roots are confined within a container. Hard pruning just before the growing season gets under way helps and makes for a healthier plant. Plumbago looks happiest when allowed to swarm over banks or walls, the ground beneath becoming dotted with a blue confetti of fallen petals. Summer jasmine (*Jasminum officinale*) can be persuaded to scramble through plumbago, adding sprays of white flowers, whose scent is so powerful that close-to it can be almost too much.

With summer growth so fast, herbaceous and even annual climbers can be blended in with the more permanent ones. Sweet peas (*Lathyrus odoratus*), if sown indoors in autumn or late winter and planted out in spring, can be made to climb through jasmine, making a rich cocktail of fragrance. On their own, however, sweet peas are best trained as cordons and pruned so that their blooms are larger and their flowering period longer. For exhibition blooms or a succession of long-stemmed flowers for arranging indoors, remove side shoots, pinch off tendrils and prevent flowers going to seed.

In greenhouse or conservatory, frost-tender hot water plants (*Achimenes*) are opening their first blooms. Grown from grub-like rhizomes, these members of the African violet family (*Gesneriaceae*), were traditionally started off by being watered with warm water. Nowadays, a couple of weeks in an electrically heated propagator does the trick. Within a couple of months of planting, the first blue or red flowers will appear, and continue all summer. The lax, flexible stems are perfect for hanging baskets or high shelves, showing off the flattened trumpet blooms. Use standard potting compost. Do not allow the temperature to fall below around 15°C (6°F).

RIGHT: *Deliciously scented, constantly blooming and simple to grow, sweet peas (*Lathyrus odoratus*) are one of the most useful of the climbing annuals.*

56

ABOVE: *The ragged flowers of* Astrantia major rubra *are darker than those of the wild*

version of this beautiful plant, which are green and white.

Among the lower-growing plants, *Astrantia major*, also known as melancholy gentleman, brings a special quality to summer borders. These are meadow plants with green-and-white, ruff-like blooms. A number of garden cultivars, identified as *A. major rubra*, have deep red blooms. Seedlings vary considerably so plant buyers need to choose carefully; named clones are safer. Of these, *A. major* 'Hadspen Blood' is one of the best, having dark stems as well as deep maroon flowers. With soft pink blooms shaped exactly like mediaeval crowns, *A. maxima* is a glorious plant for moist soil in sunshine. The tiny species *A. minor* is really an alpine. In mountain meadows it looks like myriads of tiny stars among the short grasses.

Tropical gardens invariably boast burgeoning beds of cannas, the Indian shot plant. These plants have such lush, fast-growing foliage and flowers in such strong colours of red, orange and yellow, that they are universally popular wherever frost is absent and water abundant. Even in chilly climates, they provide specimen plants for summer or dots in bedding schemes. Dark-leaved varieties such as *C.* 'Black Knight' or *C. indica* 'Purpurea' are doubly useful. Cannas do best in hot conditions in moist, fertile soil. In colder areas, they are slow starters, and need to be over-wintered under glass.

In cooler, drier conditions members of the deadnettle family (*Labiatae*), provide decorative foliage and interesting flower colours. One of the biggest genera are the sages (*Salvia*). Old World species have mainly blue flowers of varying sizes, all displaying the hooked, lipped petals of the genus. Of particular beauty are the Caucasian *S. forsskaolii*, whose pale blue-and-white flowers are flecked with rust, and various garden forms of the hybrid *S.* x *superba*, which has dark blue flower spikes. These plants look wonderful in contrast with the closely related pale buff-yellow *Phlomis russeliana*. Lavenders make excellent companions with their purple flowers and silvery foliage.

KNAUTIA MACEDONICA

Meadow flowers, with their masses of small but brightly coloured blooms, help to create an effect similar to the Impressionist painting style of pointillism, where a picture is composed of hundreds of coloured dots. If small enough, flowers with colours that might otherwise clash with a general theme can be used to enrich the groundswell of colours. With this little scabious, whose deep crimson flowers are in constant supply throughout summer, colour clashes are unlikely. Not especially long-lived as a perennial, this free seeder should develop self-maintaining colonies in a sunny border. If plants become too leggy, cut them back hard, regardless of season, and expect new growth to follow with a fresh crop of colour.

DIANTHUS BARBATUS

According to legend, the traditional 'Sweet William' was rechristened 'Stinking Billy' by supporters of the Stuart dynasty when William of Orange was brought over to England from the Netherlands to replace King James II in 1688. But call it what you like, this is a beautiful and sweetly fragrant flower which has long been a favourite with gardeners. Breeding has altered both stature and colour. Some of the finest strains are the so-called 'auricula-eyed' series which have red, pink or white centres to contrasting petal colours. Recent developments include the introduction of an annual cultivar, 'New Era', which, unlike the more usual biennial kinds, will germinate and flower in a single season.

AMMI MAJUS

One of the most architectural of plant families is *Umbelliferae*, many of whose species grow tall with ferny or feathery foliage and white, cream or yellow, umbrella-shaped umbels. With its finely divided foliage and generous, domed white flowers, *Ammi majus* is even more distinctive than Queen Anne's lace. Other members of the family which exhibit great character are *Angelica archangelica*, a monster perennial which grows to 2m (6ft), and the feathery, soft-leaved fennel. Propagate from seed.

BUDDLEJA x WEYERIANA

At the back of a sunny border, buddlejas make great companions for the bold romneyas, particularly *Buddleja x weyeriana*, whose purple-centred, apricot blooms correspond with the gold at the centres of the white poppies. It is a hybrid between the better known purple-flowered *B. davidii* and the orange, globe-flowered *B. globosa*. These shrubs need hard pruning back to less than 1m (3ft) every spring to prevent them growing coarse. In spite of such harsh treatment, they will throw out branches to almost 3m (10ft) each season. Propagate by taking cuttings in late summer or by layering.

GLAUCIUM FLAVUM

The European horned poppy has rich yellow blooms, followed by long, horn-like seed pods. A plant of the foreshore, particularly where there are shingle banks, it is easily grown from seed, requiring sharply draining conditions in full sun. Pods harvested as they ripen and stored in paper bags will split and spill seed which can be sown in spring. *Glaucium corniculatum* (syn. *G. phoenicium*), another member of the poppy family is

an inhabitant of the sand dunes and semi-deserts of the Middle East. Although the unique blue-grey of the plant's lobed foliage is its main attraction, in summer the flame-orange flowers are so vivid and cheerful that they make a pretty display in their own right, followed later by horn-like seed pods. They are wonderful contrasted with blue cornflowers (see pages 48 and 52) or the blue pimpernel (*Anagallis arvensis caerulea*).

ROSCOEA CAUTLEOIDES

The distinctive blooms of *Roscoea cautleoides* resemble orchids, but since its needs are so simple anyone can grow it. Any soil will do, even shallow chalk, in full sun, in an area that does not become too wet but does not bake too hard in the summer. Perhaps the best form is 'Kew Beauty', a large-flowered variety the colour of fresh butter. Other good species include the gorgeous purple-flowered *R. purpurea* (syn. *R. procera*).

After the irises (see pages 55 and 56) are done, colour can be continued in a dry, sunny aspect with those gems of the border, the pinks. Clove- or sweet-scented favourites among old-fashioned pinks include laced kinds such as *Dianthus* 'London Brocade' or 'Dad's Favourite', or the intensely fragrant 'Camilla', an ancient variety of obscure origin which has silver-edged maroon petals. Most *Dianthus* fare best, in well-drained, limy soil but few of the old varieties flower more than once in a season.

More recently bred border pinks often produce successions of blooms throughout summer and even occasionally during winter. A classic example found in flower shops all over the world (I have even seen it in Singapore) is 'Doris'. Soft salmon pink with a carmine eye, this is the one to choose where there is space only for a single plant. It has thrown several excellent repeat-flowering sports, of which 'Diane' is a cheerful salmon orange.

History has left us with a legacy of misnomers among plants but none has stuck more obstinately than the so-called geraniums. More correctly called pelargoniums, these are so varied in hue these days that the true 'geranium' red kind has almost been forgotten. An indication of the wild colours available is given by some of the odd-sounding names, such as 'Ringo Violet' and 'Orbit Glow'. Older kinds, with decorative leaves, are still universal favourites for mixed plantings. The red-flowered 'Dolly Varden' or salmon-shaded 'Frank Headley' are good examples. Pelargoniums enjoy hot, dry conditions, and all those mentioned here are easy to raise from cuttings which can be taken at any time during the growing season.

In situations where the loud reds and pinks of pelargoniums are too strident, *Nemesia caerulea* is a quieter alternative which enjoys the same conditions. This extraordinary perennial has sweetly fragrant, pallid lavender flowers that are constantly on view from spring to winter.

RIGHT: *The fragrant white flowers of* Romneya coulteri, *a relative of the poppy, open with puckers in their petals that are soon ironed out by the sun.*

The chief period of beauty for these remarkable

and versatile climbers is summer.

Clematis

It should be possible to have a clematis in flower for almost every month of the year in a cool or temperate garden. First come the early large-flowered hybrids, raised from such eastern species as *C. lanuginosa*. Among these are pink and lavender cultivars such as 'Nelly Moser' and many of doubles such as 'Proteus', as well as varieties mentioned on page 52. As their buds develop on the previous year's growths, these varieties must be pruned only immediately after blooming, if at all. If the plants have become troublesome and untidy, however, harder pruning, even though it may render one season's early flowers forfeit, will do the plants themselves no lasting harm at all.

Next come the later hybrids, whose blooms are still quite large but are produced after the longest day. Many are related to *C.* 'Jackmanii', one of the finest climbers in cultivation with its profusion of midnight-blue, four-sepalled flowers over many weeks. The form *C.* 'Jackmanii Alba' has white blooms, often double or semi-double, dashed with a trace of blue. *C.* 'Jackmanii Superba' is more purple in flower, with larger sepals (the coloured parts of a clematis are not petals).

Highly coloured and good natured small-flowered hybrids have been raised from a European species, *C. viticella*. The wild form has small, half-open blue blooms but for gardens there are red, purple, blue, white and bi-coloured hybrids and forms. Because they can be treated like herbaceous perennials, and cut hard back every winter, these hybrids are especially useful for growing through shrubs or small trees which might otherwise be dull in summer.

Almost without exception, clematis enjoy fertile, limy or alkaline soil which never dries out but is never waterlogged. They must have cool roots, which is easy enough to arrange by simply having plants growing at their feet or by shading their roots with mulches. Like so many climbing woodlanders, they like their flowers to be presented to the sky, rather than being overshadowed.

FROM THE TOP:

Clematis macropetala *has flowers with generous bunches of petals and stamens which have evolved to make the blooms look double.*

One of the finest of the C. viticella *hybrids, C. 'Madame Julia Correvon' produces medium-sized cherry-red blooms for months.*

One of the cleanest pinks among large-flowered clematis, C. 'Hagley Hybrid' blooms are set off by the chocolate-coloured stamens.

RIGHT: *One of the best large-flowered hybrid clematis, C. 'Jackmanii Superba' blooms soon after the longest day, continuing for months. It needs to be pruned hard in late winter.*

What a legacy we have from that great Eurasian region, the Caucasus, where iron-hard winters and a short, continental growing season have enabled the kind of herbaceous perennial to evolve which gives a speedy summer display then disappears during winter. This is a wonderful attribute in a garden plant because, like a good-natured thespian, it keeps clear of the stage while earlier colleagues are doing their act, performs with a flourish and then has the decency to make a clean exit as quickly as possible. Perfect examples are the globe thistles (*Echinops ritro*), which blend seamlessly with the hardy salvias, cranesbills and other midsummer border subjects. The lush, dark foliage of ligularias looks best when they are grown in damp, rich soil. Although slugs and snails are often troublesome, the burning orange or bright golden-yellow daisy flowers compensate. All these perennials benefit from a light dressing of feed or manure in spring.

From the Americas come the phloxes. Following the spring-flowering species (see page 41) are the grander, longer-lasting summer-flowering species such as *P. paniculata* and the more elegant *P. maculata*, with glossy foliage and pink-eyed blooms. Two of the most satisfactory cultivars of the latter are 'Alpha', pink, and 'Omega' (see left), which is white with a lilac-pink eye. *P. paniculata* is taller than these, up to 90cm (3ft), and a little coarser. Its honey scent evokes the height of summer for me, perhaps because in a flower show marquee it is more pervasive than even that of roses. There are hundreds of cultivars, though fewer now than when phloxes were the height of fashion in the 1950s and 1960s. Current favourites include the soft lilac-coloured 'Franz Schubert', 'Bright Eyes', shell pink with a carmine centre, and 'Starfire', a burning rose-red. An older classic is 'Fujiyama', a taller, more robust perennial than most phloxes with dazzling white flowers. Phloxes are happy in any soil, but dislike it too dry or hot. Feed in spring and divide every two to three years.

LEFT: *Forms of* Phlox maculata, *such as the white-flowered 'Omega' shown here, have dark, glossy foliage and generous amounts of flowers.*

SCABIOSA CAUCASICA 'Clive Greaves'

The lasting qualities of *Scabiosa caucasica* flowers, combined with their gentle blue colour and lacy shape, make them excellent for floral arrangements. In gardens, flowers are produced over most of the growing season. 'Clive Greaves' has violet-blue petals with buff, pincushion-like centres. 'Mount Cook' is a superb white form from New Zealand. To encourage flowers, feed with potassium fertilizer in spring, enrich the soil with organic mulches and keep harvesting blooms. Divide and replant every few years.

HYDRANGEA MACROPHYLLA 'Blue Wave'

When they first appear, the sterile florets, which surround the true flowers in lacecap hydrangeas like 'Blue Wave', lack colour. Pigment gradually suffuses the pallid tissue, reaching a climax of intensity as the true flowers open. When these mature at summer's end, green, bronze and purple shades develop, and the sterile florets begin to resemble ordinary leaves. As the flowers die, the leafy material becomes crisp and almost translucent, the colour of parchment. Lacecap, and mophead, hydrangeas prefer dappled shade and need cool roots, preferably in leafy woodland soil. Propagate from cuttings in summer.

FUCHSIA

While species such as the tender *Fuchsia boliviana* need a subtropical climate or the protection of a conservatory, hybrids raised from the tougher species are perfectly happy outdoors during the warmer months. Some are even frost hardy, although unlikely to survive extreme weather. Older cultivars, like red-and-damson 'Mrs Popple', the ruffled 'Dollar Princess' and dark-leaved 'Thalia', are all

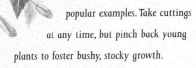

popular examples. Take cuttings at any time, but pinch back young plants to foster bushy, stocky growth.

HEMEROCALLIS 'Prima Donna'

Originating mostly from Japan, the day lilies have been crossed and selected to produce a bewildering range of colours. Apart from the garnet-coloured 'Red Precious', the most successful colours are in the yellow and orange range. The blooms of such large-flowered varieties as 'Prima Donna' often last more than a day. Although the large flowers can be dramatic, the smaller, more shapely blooms of hybrids such as 'Corky' are produced in greater numbers. The sweetly scented lemon flowers of *H. citrina* are a useful alternative to the more modern hybrids. Hemerocallis enjoy deeply dug soil that is rich in organic material. Sun or gentle shade are preferred, but avoid planting them in too hot a position.

ANTIRRHINUM

Most of the modern bedding forms of snapdragons are dwarf or semi-dwarf, and seed series include the F1 'Floral Showers' and 'Royal Carpet'. Taller varieties, such as 'Liberty Mixed' which will grow as well in a cool greenhouse as outdoors, are useful for cutting. Grown as annuals, many of the seed series are almost fully frost hardy so can be sown early in the year and bedded outside, provided they are grown hard and outside temperatures remain above -2°C (28°F). Snapdragons are prone to rust disease, which is difficult to control. If you discover rust, desist from growing snapdragons for a few years.

KNIPHOFIA 'Little Maid' and SEDUM SPECTABILE 'Brilliant'

Distinctly green in the bud, *Kniphofia* 'Little Maid' has a cool lemon-cream effect when mature. Smaller than most pokers, seldom exceeding 45cm (18in), it is valuable for use at the border front. It makes a good companion for *Sedum spectabile* 'Brilliant'. Ice plants are full of character, making a fine foliage display all summer, when the leaves are so cool looking, and then coming into colour at summer's end with coral-pink, flat-topped flower heads, which attract butterflies. 'Brilliant' has one of the strongest colours. Regular division is important, to prevent plants from becoming weakened at their centres and flopping over, a task best carried out in early spring.

There is nothing like the nose for triggering memories, but different scents have different recall for different people. Among summer's most distinctive aromas are the fruit-laden smell of the pineapple broom (*Cytisus battandieri*) and the sweet, spice-tinged fragrance of the ginger lily (*Hedychium gardnerianum*), whose handsome flower spikes are pale yellow with contrasting scarlet stigmas. Perhaps most distinctive of all is *Geranium macrorrhizum*. When brushed against, the leaves of this plant emit not merely the odour of apples, but the precise smell of an apple loft in midwinter, when a few of the fruit need to be eaten quickly because they are on the turn.

Shakespeare's 'luscious woodbine', the honeysuckle, is an essential ingredient in any planting recipe for a fragrant bower. Perfumes vary, though, and some honeysuckles have no scent at all. The old-fashioned climbing *Lonicera periclymenum* (see right) has a sweet, slightly spiced fragrance, and the form 'Graham Thomas' is one of the finest honeysuckles. Named after a great twentieth-century British plantsman, it has soft primrose-coloured flowers which deepen to straw with age to be followed by a generous crop of berries. The first honeysuckle to flower, however, is *L. periclymenum* 'Belgica' (syn. 'Early Dutch').

This is a good time of year to take stock and overhaul some plants to ensure a fresh look during the coming weeks. Some herbaceous perennials which flowered earlier and are now going to seed can be encouraged to produce a fresh crop of flowers by strategic cutting back now. Violas, for example, especially the very long-lasting *Viola cornuta* and its hybrids, will have grown leggy by now, but the straggling growths can be removed, right back to ground level. An application of feed, plus a generous watering in dry weather, will stimulate a crop of flowering stems. Some of the cranesbills respond to this treatment, particularly meadow cranesbill (*Geranium pratense*) and its relatives as well as the pink *G. endressii*.

Some of the low-growing summer-flowering shrubs also benefit from a trim in midsummer to stimulate autumn blooms, or at least a fresh crop of foliage. If, for example, you are gathering lavender either to dry or simply to use in floral arrangements, try cutting the bushes well back into the foliage to stimulate regeneration. Sage, cotton lavender and rosemary will also respond well to this treatment, as will rock roses and sun roses. Cutting tender plants back this early will ensure that regrowth has had time to harden off before the onset of winter, increasing their chances of survival.

Mophead and lacecap hydrangeas (see page 65 and 84) produce flowers not merely to contemplate, but to brood over, or at least to keep on revisiting. Apart from lasting for months, they run through a whole sequence of gentle changes, from the first swelling of the inflorescence to the final fade out in autumn (see page 65). Although hardy, these hydrangea species dislike deep frost, especially in spring when their buds are emerging. Old flowers should be clipped off and the bushes trimmed of awkward or senescent growth as soon as the new buds start to develop in spring. Take hold of the old flower and look down the stem until you find the first of the large buds. Clip just above a plump, outward facing bud, but do not cut too far back down the stem.

Old fashioned Lonicera periclymenum

has a sweet, slightly spiced fragrance.

TROPAEOLUM SPECIOSUM

Although happy growing on a wall or fence, the flame nasturtium looks best when weaving through dark evergreens. The roots appreciate the shade thrown by the foliage, but, when the top growth finally scrambles upwards to the sunshine, the flowers make a brilliant highlight on the sombre background. *Tropaeolum speciosum* can be hard to get established, but once it has settled in and, if it likes the position, seedlings will appear all over the garden. It is not, as some authorities claim, a lime hater but a plant that relishes a cool, leafy soil.

PHYGELIUS x RECTUS 'African Queen'

The colours of the southern African Cape figworts are extraordinary, especially when studied closely, for the throat of each individual tube-shaped flower is a different, contrasting colour from the outside. *Phygelius x rectus* 'African Queen' (syn. *P. aequalis* 'Indian Chief') has coral or coppery pink blooms, with canary-yellow throats. The blooms of *P. aequalis* 'Yellow Trumpet' are a more subdued primrose yellow, inside and out. With their preference for a moist site, but one that is not too shaded, these are not the easiest plants to accommodate. Where they are happy, however, they will flower incessantly throughout the summer. Cut the plants back each spring to promote new growth.

ACHILLEA 'Lachsschönheit'

Also known as *Achillea* 'Salmon Beauty', this is just one of a range of milfoils or garden yarrows with feathery foliage and flat-topped flowers in varying shades of white, cerise pink or sunset colours. Flowering at about 45cm (18in) without needing support, they make a huge contribution to a sunny border. Careful selection is needed, however, since some of the colours are muddy, especially in over-mature flowers. An older cultivar that has stood the test of time quite well is *A. millefolium* 'Cerise Queen', a strong wine pink. As most seedling selections are inferior, be sure to obtain the true cultivar, propagated vegetatively. Achilleas are surprisingly resistant to dry conditions.

Absorbing though they are, some of the daisy family (see page 71), which are so abundant at this time of year, are incredibly difficult to identify. They even succeed in keeping quite expert botanists perplexed until they have had time to carry out minute anatomical examinations of the flowers. The delectably fragrant chamomile, for example, which is lovely grown *en masse* as a lawn but just as beautiful in flower, looks rather like its evil-smelling relative, stinking mayweed (*Anthemis cotula*). And European corn marigolds (*Anthemis*) could be easily mistaken for some of the southern African wild daisies, while certain wild dahlias masquerade as perennial species of bidens.

Set apart from the general run of daisy flowers are those special plants with star quality. *Cosmos atrosanguineus*, for instance, with its deep maroon to black, chocolate-scented flowers is far prettier than any of the dahlias, except perhaps for the hybrid *D.* 'Bishop of Llandaff', whose bronze to black leaves make such a wonderful foil for the burning scarlet of its flowers. The Chilean species *Grindelia chiloensis* protects its emerging bright yellow flowers with a white, glutinous substance that is as sticky as birdlime, and is curious rather than pretty. With its startling, burning hue, *Gazania krebsiana*, which grows wild in the Namibian and south-west African semi-desert, is one of the most exciting daisy species.

Twining plants are useful for the element of surprise their travelling stems can provide. A good example is *Tropaeolum speciosum*, the South American climber. Given the right conditions, this plant will conceal its whereabouts with deceptive modesty until midsummer when suddenly a flaming red garland will appear as if from nowhere. Other valuable tropaeolum species include the orange-and-red *T. tuberosum*, the startling yellow, ground-creeping *T. polyphyllum*, which must have full sun, and, of course, the jolly annual nasturtium, *T. majus*. All like a cool, leafy soil.

ABOVE: *The dark, bewitching foliage of Dahlia 'Preston Park' makes a perfect background for the profusion of vivid scarlet blooms borne in late summer.*

The little white daisies that pop up in lawns

during endless sunny days of summer are just one

of a huge family

Daisies

ABOVE: *Marguerites* (Argyranthemum frutescens) *are easy to reproduce from cuttings and grow quickly.*

BELOW: *One of the best of the blue southern African daisies,* Felicia amelloides *'Santa Anita' is very perennial, though not hardy.*

BOTTOM: *The southern African arctotis tribe come in a burning colour range. This one is appropriately named A. 'Torch'.*

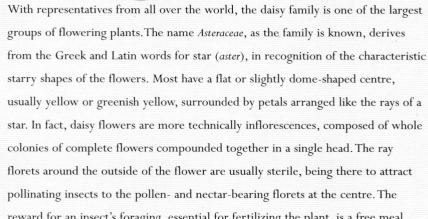

With representatives from all over the world, the daisy family is one of the largest groups of flowering plants. The name *Asteraceae*, as the family is known, derives from the Greek and Latin words for star (*aster*), in recognition of the characteristic starry shapes of the flowers. Most have a flat or slightly dome-shaped centre, usually yellow or greenish yellow, surrounded by petals arranged like the rays of a star. In fact, daisy flowers are more technically inflorescences, composed of whole colonies of complete flowers compounded together in a single head. The ray florets around the outside of the flower are usually sterile, being there to attract pollinating insects to the pollen- and nectar-bearing florets at the centre. The reward for an insect's foraging, essential for fertilizing the plant, is a free meal.

Colour, size and shape varies considerably among different daisy flowers, and the characteristic shape is often repeated in unrelated genera, for example the mesembryanthemums (Livingstone daisies) and even anemones such as *A. blanda* and *A. appenina*. Among true members of *Asteraceae*, however, probably the most frequently occuring colours are white, orange or yellow hues, although there are hundreds of examples of other colours. The southern African genus *Felicia*, has mainly blue-rayed species, usually with yellow centres. *Crepis rubra*, a hardy annual, comes in a delicate shade of pink. Osteospermums are often mauve or deep purple. Dendranthemas (the more correct name for chrysanthemums) (see page 99) come in almost any shade yellow, bronze, pink and red. From North America, the Michaelmas daisies hybrids are mauve, lavender-blue, purple or pink.

Many of the daisy tribe are either herbaceous perennials, such as *Aster amellus*, *Inula magnifica* and *Gaillardia* x *grandiflora*, or annuals like pot marigolds, Swan River daisies (*Brachyscome*) and sunflowers. There are plenty of shrubs, daisy bushes such as *Olearia* x *macrodonta* and even climbing plants, including *Senecio scandens*.

71

LEFT: *The mixed seed series* Brachyscome *'Summer Skies', a Swan River daisy, comes in a harmonized range of blues, purple blues and near white.*

Although summer has not yet fully run her course, there is a distinctly autumnal feel to the early mornings now. Dew takes longer to blow dry, the temperature climbs a little more slowly and there is more moisture in the air both early and late in the day. Plants that stood still during dry weather begin to move again. Certain trees, particularly if there has been rain, may produce new leaves and even new branches. A few are still in flower: the hoherias, whose white blossoms look more like spring blooms, are at their climax on acid soil in sheltered gardens where frost and extreme heat are rare. Eucryphias, too, are in full glory, their white waxy flowers reminiscent of single-flowered camellias.

The best colour, at summer's end comes from the mixed flower borders. The 'short-day' osteospermums limit their blooms to spring and autumn so they should be full of bud now, ready for a final flourish when they will make great companions to perennial asters. Red hot poker (*Kniphofia*) flowers should be approaching their best period, with such varieties as the cream 'Little Maid' (see page 66) or beige-and-primrose 'Toffee Nosed' making a pale contrast with the warmer apricot shade of *K. galpinii* or the orange *K.* 'Alcazar'. Late-summer bulbs include the dramatically coloured *Tigridia*, some of the later gladiolus species and the marvel of Peru or four o'clock plant (*Mirabilis jalapa*) whose blossoms open in late afternoon to fade next day between breakfast and lunch. Mirabilis comes in several startling shades from deep yellow to shocking pink, sometimes with two jarring colours on the same plant, which is interesting, if not aesthetic.

Even though frost may not be far away, well-fed and well-tended containers still have weeks of life left in them, especially if they are fed regularly. For example, *Convolvulus sabatius* flowers every day, trailing over the sides of the containers, perhaps even taking root in the ground below and scrambling about until a mat of blue flowers develops.

LEFT: *Extensive breeding over the past century has produced dahlias in excessive sizes and outlandish colours. D. 'Senzoe Julie' is just one example.*

PROTEA REPENS

The common sugarbush is a native of the specialist habitats of southern Africa known as Fynbos, pronounced 'fain boce' and meaning 'fine bush'. There, winter rainfall ensures a plentiful water supply, even in the sharply drained volcanic sands that so many proteas grow in, but summers are hot and dry. There are 380 wild proteas, the great majority of which occupy a relatively small area. They are difficult to grow artificially, except in a subtropical or Mediterranean climate. In a roomy conservatory, however, in a sharp, sandy, acidic compost, evergreen *Protea repens* is the species to try.

TAGETES ERECTA

Although it is universally known as the African marigold, the annual *Tagetes erecta* actually comes from Central America, where it was discovered by the Spanish during their conquest of Latin America. In cultivation ever since, modern varieties bear little resemblance to the original wild plants apart from the unmistakeable aroma and shape of the leaves. Flower sizes are also much larger these days, up to 13cm (5in) across. Colours range from intense orange, through shades of yellow, pale lemon and cream. These annuals are easy to raise from seed sown frost free in early spring.

73

HEDYCHIUM x RAFILII

The ginger lilies, so called because they belong to the same family, *Zingiberaceae*, as the spices ginger and cardamom, are good as foliage plants and for their glorious flower spikes. The commonest and easiest to grow is *Hedychium gardnerianum*, whose dainty primrose-yellow flowers are made all the more dramatic by vivid scarlet stamens. The sweet fragrance of the flowers has gingery undertones so that smelling them actually makes your mouth water. *H.* x *raffilii* is a cross between *H. gardnerianum* and *H. coccineum* and is a warm orange. Ginger lilies prefer rich, leafy soil and a plentiful supply of moisture in partial shade. They are not frost hardy, so roots need to be protected in winter. Alternatively, the plants can be grown indoors.

PAPAVER SOMNIFERUM, ROSA and
SALVIA SCLARIA TURKESTANICA

Maturing opium poppies (*Papaver somniferum*), many of which are going to seed, roses and the flower spikes of *Salvia sclaria turkestanica* provide a lazy, blowsy ensemble of late summer colours. Such a group may represent a decline in the season, yet they retain great beauty, and when the last of the poppy petals have fallen, the shapely seed capsules will remain to provide a pleasing outline for weeks to come. They can even be left to provide a profile through the winter. The roses will continue to flower for many more weeks, especially if they are given a late season feed, either sprayed on as a foliar boost or sprinkled at their roots.

ACACIA PUDICA

A close relative of the yellow mimosa, which is used as a cut bloom in spring, the sensitive plant grows all over the tropics. The ferny-looking, very finely divided, leaves wilt suddenly whenever the plant is brushed against. 'Pudica' means 'shame' or 'ashamed' in Latin, as if the plant is embarrassed when touched. These plants will not tolerate night temperatures below around 13°C (55°F), but they are easy to raise from seed.

HOHERIA LYALLII

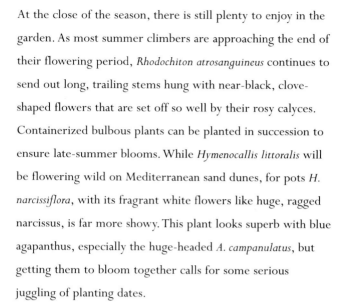

Hoherias are valuable because they come into their glory at a time of year when flowering trees are scarce. They are rapidly growing trees with large, glossy foliage, sometimes paler below than above. In late summer they are covered in a profusion of brilliant white flowers. *H. lyallii* has grey-green leaves and a spreading habit. Hoherias are suitable for warmer areas, where winter frosts are light and few and far between. They need lime-free soil and a plentiful supply of moisture.

At the close of the season, there is still plenty to enjoy in the garden. As most summer climbers are approaching the end of their flowering period, *Rhodochiton atrosanguineus* continues to send out long, trailing stems hung with near-black, clove-shaped flowers that are set off so well by their rosy calyces. Containerized bulbous plants can be planted in succession to ensure late-summer blooms. While *Hymenocallis littoralis* will be flowering wild on Mediterranean sand dunes, for pots *H. narcissiflora*, with its fragrant white flowers like huge, ragged narcissus, is far more showy. This plant looks superb with blue agapanthus, especially the huge-headed *A. campanulatus*, but getting them to bloom together calls for some serious juggling of planting dates.

Although it will be a week or two before the main Michaelmas daisy season is under way, a number of early asters are already in full bloom. Nothing looks more glorious on a misty late summer morning than sunlight shining on their mauve, purple or pink flowers, the focus softened by the overnight dew. *Aster × frikartii* is one of the most decorative of the earlier forms, especially the variety known as 'Mönch', whose soft, lavender-blue rays contrast so beautifully with the greenish-yellow flower centres.

If the tree mallows were cut back in midsummer to stimulate fresh blooms, they will be back to full power now, and should continue to flower uproariously until the frost. One of the most popular, *Lavatera* 'Barnsley' has white to pale pink blooms with deep pink centres. It sometimes reverts to the original, more uniform pink of its parent. When it does, I can never decide whether to excise the reversion or let it take over the plant, as there is much to be said for both forms.

By now, some of the more tender Central and South American salvias will have grown into sizeable shrubs and will be coming into flower. Of these, one of the more interesting is *S. guaranitica*, which, in the absence of frost to knock it

back, develops into a great gangling monster, excellent for the back of a border where it can flop about without making a mess. The flowers are a sombre dusky purple or blue. Once they appear, they will stay for a long while. In cold areas, though, it may not flower soon enough and could be overtaken by the impending autumn frosts.

With these colourful flowers, summer does not so much come to an end as merge imperceptibly with autumn. The equinox, after which nights grow increasingly longer than days, is merely a date. Weather patterns, even though change may be in the air, can often lag behind the date, giving a remission from colder weather. There may even be an Indian summer to extend the season. But even when autumn threatens with gales or cold wet weather, if you garden wisely, you will still be spoilt for choice when you venture outside each day to select a new flower.

The tree mallow Lavatera *'Barnsley'*
provides a colourful shower of blooms.

75

ABOVE: *During the early weeks of autumn, the colours of mophead hydrangea blooms gradually fade, taking on attractive reddish and bronze tints.*

The season of mists brings with it a bounteous harvest, not only of fruits but of an unimaginable wealth of seasonal flowers

Autumn

Harvest time. In spite of the declining days and resulting gentle slide towards the end of the growing season, the abundance of autumn plant material defies belief. This is a period of plenty when well-planted gardens are more full of potential than at any other time of year. Fruit is ripening yet the quantity of flowers continues to grow and expand as if winter could never come. In addition to the hundreds of late-summer blooms spilling over the seasonal divide there is a developing collection of autumn flowers with colours to harmonize with the newly formed berries and changing foliage colours.

RIGHT: *With clusters of globular deep red flowers, the coral plant (*Berberidopsis corallina*), a climber, brings late colour to a sheltered spot.*

FAR RIGHT: Clerodendrum trichotomum fargesii *bears blue berries that are every bit as attractive as the fragrant white flowers which preceded them.*

*Cooler, longer nights bring a whole
new tribe of plants into bloom as
the short-day plants begin to flower and carry
the season into winter*

Autumn bounty

Autumn begins as a period of transition. At the time of the autumnal equinox summer flowers usually have plenty of mileage left in them. In many areas frost is unlikely for a few weeks, and even where there has been a gale or a rainy spell, a renewed warm period brings a remission.

Late summer tiredness in flower borders is revitalized in autumn by the cooler nights and shorter days. After weeks of standing still such late season plants as asters, dendranthemas and some of the crocosmias are stimulated to bloom. In a well-planned garden they will all arrive together with a floursih of colour to round off the growing season. Warm colours work particularly well at this time of year, especially reds, oranges and russets which harmonize so well with foliage colours as they change from predominantly green to yellow, gold and on through the fiery shades of the season. Plants with fresh green foliage stand out too, particularly sedums with their fleshy leaves and bright coral flowers, hot-coloured kniphofias, and tall-growing Japanese anemones, whose leaves seem to stay fresh even in a drought.

In contrast with the warmness of the autumnal tints, many of the perennial asters have lavender, blue or mauve shades. Cooler, more intense blues can be found in the strange, three-petalled flowers of *Commelina coelestis*, a close relative of the coarser, darker, spidery-flowered tradescantias, and the fascinating range of later-flowering gentians. Although the gentians tend to be difficult to grow and therefore frequently limited to being collectors' plants, the colour combinations they effect, especially when planted with shrubs whose foliage creates a good autumnal display, are so sumptuous that the plants are worth persevering with.

Autumn surprises come from bulbs, many of which send up rapidly developing flowers, held on naked stems. Big pink flowers of *Amaryllis*

belladonna, for example, appear from nowhere. Although more dramatic in appearance, they are less elegant than the nerines, whose curled and crimped petals are perfect for indoor floral arrangements. Even in very cold areas there are colchicums springing leafless out of the turf. In shade, the tiny pink flowers of cyclamen species appear. Autumn-flowering snowdrops can create a false impression of spring, especially if they are planted with the beautiful *Sternbergia lutea*, which resembles a small daffodil.

Then, as the days shorten at an accelerating rate, the first frosts come and sharpen the colours of the trees and shrubs. At their feet are brightly coloured carpets of fallen leaves. Even when the days have become too cold to venture outdoors without wrapping up, there will still be plenty to see. Dendranthemas braving the frost and rain, the first camellia, the last rose, a confused primrose that popped up too early, or even a dahlia that managed to dodge the frost in a really sheltered spot to struggle out with a final flower.

79

LEFT: *Cinerarias, such as this* Senecio x hybridus *'Cindi', are a valuable source of late colour.*

ABOVE: Colchicum speciosum *'Album'*. ABOVE RIGHT: Prunus subhirtella *'Autumnalis'*.

CALLISTEMON CITRINUS

Bottlebrush trees, particularly the species *Callistemon citrinus*, have a long flowering period, often producing their first blooms in spring, continuing through summer into early autumn. None of them is truly hardy, but *C. citrinus* tolerates temperatures very close to freezing over short periods, and can even survive a coating of hoar frost provided the air temperature is not too cold for too long. These members of the eucalyptus family occur naturally in moist Australian heathland and perform best when the roots do not dry out too severely. The hard brown fruits of preceding seasons occur at intervals along the stems. In the wild, these are retained until soon after the plant is affected by bush fires, when they will be shed ready to germinate as part of the natural regeneration process.

LOBELIA TUPA

What a large and varied genus are the lobelias. And what could look less like the familiar, low-growing blue bedding plant than *Lobelia tupa* with its huge, furry leaves and 2m (6ft) spikes of blood-red flowers, like rows of hooked tiger claws arranged up the stems. A native of Chile, *L. tupa* enjoys moist, rich soil in a sheltered spot. The species is barely frost hardy and therefore needs a dry mulch over the roots in winter, to prevent them from freezing.

ALLIUM CHRISTOPHII

Like most members of the onion and garlic tribe, *Allium christophii* flowers in late spring or early summer. In autumn the developing seed heads have as much beauty as the silvery lilac blooms, and later, when they have turned brown and crisp, they will retain their elegant globe shapes. *A. christophii* is a good species for naturalizing, sometimes producing flowering-sized bulbs within a single year. On light, friable soils, the species will create its own self-perpetuating colonies without further help.

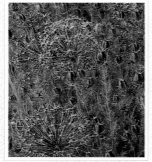

The fiery blooms of the crocosmias complement the yellowing foliage of the trees and shrubs. Wild species such as *Crocosmia paniculata* and *C. masoniorum* have been used to develop some glorious garden hybrids whose flowers range in colour from pale lemon to vivid scarlet. Some have especial character: the blooms of *C.* 'Jackanapes' are startling scarlet orange and yellow; *C.* 'Solfaterre' has warm yellow blooms set off by khaki foliage; and among larger-flowered kinds, *C.* 'Emily McKenzie' has warm orange petals with darker, brownish bases. Although they come from such warm mountain regions as the South African Drakensberg, crocosmias prefer moist but free-draining soil with plenty of organic material worked in. In cold regions, it is advisable to protect their corms from excessive frost using a dry mulch, and to defer cutting back dead stems until spring.

Among herbaceous plants with huge, dramatic leaves and conspicuous flowers at this time of year are the larger tobacco plants. Most of the popular hybrids have been raised from *Nicotiana affinis*, the evening-scented species, whose blooms turn limp by day but revive after dark to produce a strong fragrance. More spectacular is *N. sylvestris*, a vast tender perennial which, in deep, rich soil in a warm spot, will tower to almost 2m (6ft) with broad, somewhat glutinous foliage and sprays of long, curved, tubular flowers of pure white. The quantity of dust-fine seed that each plant can produce is prodigious, but you need save only a pinch to sow under glass in early spring in case the parent succumbs to the winter.

Few trees flower at summer's end, but the exceptions are so notable and so distinctive as to be worth collecting. The eucryphias, spring-like in appearance with waxy blooms so reminiscent of single white camellias, are spectacular in early autumn and flower for many weeks. Originating from South America, they are barely frost hardy, and although moderately lime tolerant, they prefer acid, sandy soil in full light.

ABOVE: *Natives of southern Africa, the crocosmias, such as this rich red C. 'Lucifer',*

contribute hot hues and cool elegance to the autumn garden.

A shrub that enjoys similar conditions to the huge tobaccos (see page 80), and which makes a good companion plant, is *Clerodendrum trichotomum fargesii* (see left), whose odd-smelling white flowers give way at this time of year to greenish blue-black berries made all the more beautiful by the brilliant pink calyces which remain after the petals have fallen and are every bit as lovely as flowers.

In spite of its relatively small stature, *C. trichotomum* is easy to train into the dimensions and outline of a tree, which can be useful in small spaces requiring a good focal point. One of the less vigorous herbaceous climbers can be grown through mature specimens to heighten the effect. The elegant *Clematis texensis* 'Etoile Rose', the highly coloured *Eccremocarpus scaber* or, perhaps, one of the perennial sweet peas are all suitable.

At ground level, this is gentian time. European species tend to flower in spring, but a choice, mostly autumn-flowering selection comes from China and the Himalayas. From the light, electric hues of *Gentiana farreri* to the deep peacock-blue radiance of *G. sino-ornata*, these plants have a special place in the hearts of most plantsmen. Tall, herbaceous European species include *G. asclepiadea*, which has deep blue trumpet blooms arranged along a 60cm (2ft) stem. Among named forms *G.* 'Alba' is white, and *G.* 'Knightshayes' is dark blue with a white throat. If you plant a selection of these named forms then allow a colony of seedlings to develop undisturbed, quite a number of different colours and characters will arise.

Gentians can be rather demanding, but will thrive in the right conditions. Most prefer moist or even wet soil, especially where there is a very high level of organic matter mixed in with the loam. Some are lime-haters. *G. sino-ornata* likes precisely the same conditions as most rhododendrons, that is, cool, moist roots but enough sunshine to promote flowers. *G. farreri* prefers limestone soil but hates it too dry.

LEFT: *Almost as conspicuous as the flowers, the glossy fruits of the shrub* Clerodendrum trichotomum fargesii *are set off by pinkish calyces.*

GENTIANA ASCLEPIADEA

Gentiana asclepiadea, a European species, grows taller than its prostrate mountain cousins, but the flowers nonetheless carry the intense blue colouring and trumpet shapes that typify the genus. Sometimes these plants are difficult to establish, perhaps because they need to acquire the right kinds of micro-organisms close to their roots to assist with nutrient exchange. Once they begin to thrive, they multiply steadily and can form sizeable colonies over a number of years.

GENTIANA x STEVENAGENSIS

Bred from the wild *Gentiana sino-ornata* in the early part of this century at the famous Six Hills Nursery in Britain, *G.* x *stevenagensis* is a fine garden variety. It prefers acid or neutral soil, preferably with a high peat content, in well-lit conditions that are not too baking hot. Propagation is best done by division soon after flowering in autumn. Sometimes, the plant literally falls apart when lifted, providing plenty of fragments for replanting.

GENTIANA PARADOXA

Among Asian species of gentian, *Gentiana paradoxa* is attractive in foliage as well as in flower. The leaves are darker green and more slender than those of most of the autumn-flowering gentians. They crowd along the stems, which tend to stand more erect than those of *G. sino-ornata*, presenting the flowers at their ends more prominently. Flower colour is as intense a blue as in any gentian, with each bloom striped on its outside in alternating beige and navy blue to black. As with all gentians, cool, moist soil is preferred, but never saturated. In the wild, most of the Asian species inhabit the turf of mountain meadows where soil is full of organic matter and damp but free draining.

ANEMONE x HYBRIDA and A. HUPEHENSIS

The late-flowering anemones *Anemone x hybrida* and *A. hupehensis* come from China where they have been featured in gardens for centuries. Tough, vigorous and indiscriminate about where they grow, even tolerating extreme drought and dense shade, these are the lazy gardener's dream plants. They begin flowering profusely in late summer, heralding the main flush of autumn perennials. Their colours are gentle, being various shades of pink, from pale shell to rich purplish cerise, and white. There are many named cultivars including soft pink *A. hupehensis* 'September Charm', the deeper semi-double *A. hupehensis japonica* (syn. *A. x hybrida*) 'Bressingham Glow' and pure white *A. x hybrida* 'Honorine Jobert'.

HYDRANGEA MACROPHYLLA 'Europa'

From the moment their first flowers appear until the last days of autumn, beautiful mophead hydrangeas display subtly shifting colours. During the height of the growing season, the rounded inflorescences glow with strong shades of blue, reddish or purplish pink, shades of salmon or white. As the days shorten, the flowers do not die but rather their colours slip into a declining intensity, gradually adopting the bronze and blush overtones of autum. The foliage also moves through similar colour changes, deepening in hue until the whole appearance of the plant has shifted from flower and leaf in strongly contrasting hues to a soft suffusion of warmer tones.

LOPHOSPERMUM ERUBESCENS

Herbaceous climbers such as *Lophospermum erubescens* provide speedy colour, and are especially useful for weaving through more permanent wall plants where they can alleviate dull periods. A member of the foxglove family, *L. erubescens* has trumpet-shaped blooms in exactly the same glowing pink of an autumn sunrise. This perennial is easy to raise from seed sown in gentle heat in late winter or early spring.

Summer may be over but days are still warm, and the summer annuals still have several weeks to run before setting their final seeds. Given continued warmth and a plentiful supply of rain, such annuals as cornflowers, larkspurs, pot marigolds and poppies will flower generously until the first frosts. Cosmos, the South American roadside plant, is particularly long lasting if fed and watered regularly and will continue to produce bloom after bloom in pink, wine-red, white or candy stripes, all set off by filigree foliage so soft and lacy that one cannot resist stroking it. Extra sowings of most hardy annuals in late spring or early summer will guarantee an extended autumn display, especially if the seedlings are thinned after emerging to about 30cm (12in) apart and if they are grown in deeply worked, fertile ground to which a general fertilizer has been added.

This is a good time, too, for the later-flowering lilies, many of which are fine for growing in containers or among shrubs. Many species are fully lime tolerant. *Lilium henryi*, for instance, prefers limy conditions and in fertile soil grows up to 2m (6ft). It bears sprays of flowers with soft apricot-orange petals curved elegantly back to reveal the prominent stamens and stigmas. The black-spotted, reddish orange tiger lily (*L. lancifolium*) thrives in any reasonable soil, even if fairly dry in summer, and obligingly produces tiny bulblets in its leaf axils which can be used to produce more plants. The sharp yellow form of *L. lancifolium* 'Luteum' is useful for creating a stronger contrast with, say, the vivid blue flowers of *Ceratostigma willmottianum* or the odd late bloom of ceanothus. Other late lily species, such as *L. auratum* and many of the hybrids, are happier in neutral or slightly acid soil. With white, cream, rose-pink or yellow petals, often with subtle suffusions of colour running through their blooms and almost always with a heady fragrance, they make a glorious display among shrubs, particularly late-blooming hydrangeas.

ABOVE: *Hybrid lilies such as Lilium 'Star Gazer', so called because the flowers tend to be held erect, have lasting qualities as cut blooms, with rich fragrance and strong colouring.*

The lilies (see page 84) are special blooms, star performers to be enjoyed as soloists or small, choice ensembles, but for sheer volume of flower goldenrod can be almost as spectacular. It grows wild in North American grasslands, the vast numbers turning the whole landscape yellow in late summer and early autumn. Looked at individually, the flowers of such species as *Solidago canadensis* are rather ordinary, but in wide drifts creating a golden tide that rises to the knees of trees and shrubs, they are spectacular. And when lit by a setting sun, they give a special Midas effect.

In gardens, goldenrods are easy, if slightly invasive perennials, happy in moderate or even poor soil but better in colour and flower if fed in spring. In very dry conditions, the plants are unlikely to die but can be so badly disfigured by mildew that you almost wish they would. The best way of countering mildew attacks is to ensure moisture-retentive soil, preferably improved with mulches, and to have healthy, young plants obtained by lifting and dividing clumps every few years. Besides the usual dark or mustard-yellow kinds of solidago, there are paler varieties, such as the lemon-coloured *S. virgaurea* 'Pale Yellow', and those whose individual florets are a touch larger and therefore more readily recognizable as being members of the aster family. A lower-growing variety is *S.* 'Goldenmosa', whose blooms give a more intensely yellow effect because the tiny flower stems are yellow as well.

Cooler nights, perhaps a short rainy spell or possibly the first of the autumn mists will bring vigour back to pots, window boxes and other containers planted with summer flowers. Even when watered regularly and fed generously, such containers can sometimes flag during a particularly hot summer, possibly because the roots of the plants get too warm to be able to function effectively. With the arrival of cooler nights, such plants as trailing lobelia, pelargoniums, petunias, fuchsias and begonias can take on a new lease of life.

LEFT: *One of the finest golden forms of goldenrod,* Solidago *'Goldenmosa' is sturdy enough to stand on its own without support, and it is not too tall.*

BERBERIDOPSIS CORALLINA

Some of the loveliest climbers grace the walls of climatically favoured gardens in late summer and early autumn. In a sheltered spot, protected from both winds and too much direct sunshine, the coral plant carries small pendent sprays of rich red blooms, looking a little like those of berberis, set off by vivid evergreen foliage. Flowering continues well into autumn, particularly if these plants are grown in lime-free soil.

Prune in early spring. This climber has limited frost tolerance only.

SCHISANDRA RUBRIFLORA

As its name suggests, the flowers of *Schisandra rubriflora* are red, but what a vivid, glowing shade of red. Although the elegant, cup-shaped or rounded flowers of this deciduous climber are produced in early summer, on female plants they are followed in autumn by a crop of deeper red fruits which provide a second display of colour. To ensure fruits are formed, male and female plants need to be grown in close proximity.

87

ALSTROEMERIA PSITTACINA

Some species of the vividly coloured South American princess lilies flower in bursts from midsummer well into autumn. Most of the varieties in cultivation result from the hybridization of several species, but one of the most interestingly coloured is *Alstroemeria psittacina*, whose red, green and black colouring is reminiscent of the parrot species which inhabit the same continent. Although barely frost hardy, these plants are easy to over-winter, provided their roots are protected from the worst of the weather using dry mulches or bulky coverings of straw or bracken. Divide the tubers to multiply the plants, but try not to disturb the roots more than once every three or more years.

CORREA 'Marion's Marvel'

The correas have great character, especially *Correa* 'Marion's Marvel'. These are tender or near tender evergreen shrubs but they are worth trying to grow in a warm and sheltered garden for the beauty of the tubular flowers. These are produced in summer, autumn and winter in gentle reds and greenish yellows. Acid soil is essential for the health of these shrubs as is shelter from the wind for their survival.

CLEMATIS 'Bill Mackenzie'

One of the most widespread and varied of plant genera, clematis comes in most colours of the spectrum. Several species, particularly those from Asia, have a unique flower texture. On *Clematis* 'Bill Mackenzie' the waxy-looking yellow flowers are reminiscent of quartered lemon or orange peel. They look thick and stiff, but the sepals are surprisingly soft to the touch. Although produced in a long succession from around the longest

day until the beginning of autumn, individual blooms are not especially long lived. Later in autumn, as flower production falters, the plants are furnished with a profusion of silky, feathery seed heads which persist through much of the winter. Other fine 'orange-peel' clematis include *C. tangutica*, whose flowers are as yellow as *C.* 'Bill Mackenzie' but more lantern-shaped, and the parchment-coloured *C. serratifolia*, whose flowers come all in a rush and are soon over but whose seed heads stay white and fluffy for months.

COLCHICUM SPECIOSUM 'Album'

Crocus-like in shape but unrelated, the colchicums erupt from the ground in early autumn without leaves. The largest-flowered species is *Colchicum speciosum*, a dramatic plant with purple- to pink-flushed blooms which reach almost 24cm (9in) and are produced in generous clusters from mature bulbs. *C. speciosum* 'Album' is a superb white form while 'Waterlily' is a large, lilac-flowered double form. The leaves follow in spring, reaching up to 60cm (2ft). To create more plants, divide the bulbs every few seasons once the flowers have begun to fade but before they have disappeared.

Climbers continue to give autumn joy, especially those whose fruits and seed capsules add to the display. Late-flowering clematis, particularly the oriental orange-peel kinds, are almost as pretty with their fluffy seed heads as with the flowers, which in some varieties keep coming until the first heavy frosts. Some of the large-flowered clematis and the viticella hybrids continue to show colour, blending with late honeysuckle flowers as well as their scarlet berries.

At ground level, there is plenty of colour still to come from diascias and the closely related, long-lived *Nemesia caerulea*. The gentle mauve, apricot and pink shades of these southern African plants blend as sweetly with autumn colours as with the sharper, cleaner hues of early summer. To keep them young and beautiful it pays to remove old flowering stems throughout the growing season as soon as they fade. An alternative treatment is to give the plants a more severe 'haircut' at the height of summer, thus shocking them into producing a new flush of fresh flowering stems. Apply a little liquid feed or potassium-rich fertilizer to stimulate extra flower production. Other plants which benefit greatly from such an enforced flowering break include perennial violas, gaillardias and many of the campanulas.

In cold gardens tender shrubs will look beautiful for several weeks to come but need placing in a protected place before the first severe frosts arrive. The big tree daturas, which grow several metres tall in open ground, can be kept to a manageable size when containerized. Under protection, their huge, dangling, fragrant blooms will keep on flowering through most of winter and benefit from continued feeding as long as they are in bloom. The royal blue flowers of *Tibouchina* have weeks to run, too, but eventually the plants will benefit from being pruned back, ready for storing over winter in a frost-free greenhouse. Even in tropical gardens, such plants can benefit from an enforced rest period.

ABOVE: *Although technically winter blooming, Viola 'Cream Princess' flowers copiously throughout autumn, sporadically during winter and freely again in spring.*

The aster season is long, up to half a year if you include the early summer bloomers, but the great majority of these gently coloured, easily grown and adaptable plants are at their best from the autumn equinox until the beginning of winter. Although mostly North American in origin, perennial asters, or Michaelmas daisies, have been developed, selected and hybridized so extensively during the past century that they have become one of the mainstays of the autumnal display all over the temperate world. Growing wild in their North American homeland, along woodland edges, roadsides or in broader drifts on the prairies, their soft mauve, blue and pinkish purple hues complement the season's changing foliage colours perfectly. Most have yellow, greenish or golden flower centres, echoing the yellowing leaves on plants around them. Some grow very tall, others stay compact with a myriad tiny flowers creating a mist of pastel colours, but the prettiest of all present their flowers in horizontal tiers.

The spotted blooms of Tricyrtis formosana *give rise to its colloquial name toad lily.*

Among the earliest to flower is *Aster amellus*, a relatively compact species seldom exceeding 45cm (18in) in height with yellow-centred, blue flowers up to 4cm (1⅓in) across. Cultivars that have stood the test of time and perform well include 'King George', with extra large, dark blue flowers; 'Pink Zenith', whose less regularly shaped blooms are a rosy magenta; and the relatively low-growing pink 'Sonia'.

The most popular of the traditional Michaelmas daisies were raised from a species found wild in New York State, *Aster novi-belgii*. Single and double varieties were raised from the tall, blue-flowered plants in colours ranging from deep royal blue, through shades of pink, powder blue, soft mauve and white. There are tall forms, reaching more than 1m (3ft), and tiny, domed dwarf varieties developed for use as border edge plants. Unfortunately, all forms of *Aster novi-belgii*, gorgeous though they undoubtedly are, have one serious failing: mildew. Furthermore, the disease appears to have been affecting them more in recent decades and, with the choice of effective fungicides becoming ever more limited for private gardeners, it makes sense to forgo such ravishing varieties and to investigate disease-resistant alternatives.

Happily, there are plenty of disease-proof asters. Nearest, perhaps, to the mainstream hybrids are cultivars raised from the New England aster (*A. novae-angliae*). Taller and coarser in the leaf, these have larger flowers and create a dramatic display. There are no clear blues, alas, but vivid pinks in such varieties as 'Harrington's Pink' and the startling cerise 'Andeken an Alma Pötschke'. The wild species is pinkish purple and worth growing, and there is a white form called 'September Snow'.

Lower growing but as gorgeous in late autumn as any flower in the border, are the forms of *A. ericoides*, whose minute individual flowers are produced in their thousands. These are long lasting and superb for cutting. They make pretty companions to another small-flowered hybrid, *A. lateriflorus*, whose tiny flush-white blooms have deeper pink centres and stay in colour right up to the end of the growing season, when in their last few weeks they contrast with foliage that has turned deep purple red.

Although strictly summer rather than autumn flowers, we cannot leave the asters without mention of perhaps the prettiest of all, *A. x frikartii* and its cultivars. These were raised by the German breeder Frikart and named after various Alpine summits. The loveliest of these is 'Mönch', whose blooms have soft, blue to mauve outer rays.

Quite unrelated to asters, and from opposite sides of the world, the toad lilies, *Tricyrtis formosana* and related species, make happy companion plants. Their glossy foliage sets off the more roughened leaves of some of the asters, and the flowers, with their somewhat liverish markings and intriguing shapes, make a comfortable association. Set among asters, in rich, leafy soil that does not dry out too much, toad lilies enjoy the shelter and shade they provide.

During a very dry, hot summer both asters and toad lilies will appreciate an occasional soaking, or will perform better if the border soil has been dressed with a generous mulch of compost, bark chips or any other bulky organic material. Asters will perform well only if lifted and divided regularly, every three years at least. In windy or exposed areas they will need support. A fungicide regime is essential for keeping *A. novi-belgii* hybrids disease free.

ASTER NOVI-BELGII 'Remembrance'

Among the finest cultivars of *Aster novi-belgii*, 'Remembrance' has large elegant sprays of semi-double purple-blue flowers on relatively tall stems. Mildew can be problematical with many cultivars of the species, but the disease will be reduced if the plants are grown in deeply dug, well-fed and well-watered soil. A prophylactic regime of recommended fungicide sprays will also help to control the problem.

ASTER AMELLUS 'Rudolph Goethe'

One of earlier cultivars, *Aster amellus* 'Rudolph Goethe' links the summer display with autumn. Although relatively low growing, its stems can be rather lax and the plants therefore benefit from a certain amount of support, especially where not grown in full sunlight. The foliage is broader than on larger asters and the stems are rougher to the touch but this is still a fine summer plant for cutting or for the outdoor display.

91

ASTER ERICOIDES 'Blue Star'

The tiny-flowered *Aster ericoides* varieties live truly up to their name, since their flowers look not only like stars (aster is Greek for star), but are produced in positive galaxies. Grouped with larger-bloomed varieties, they give a change in character, with their softer drifts, and are especially effective at the base of a border tree. Regular division and generous feeding is as important with these varieties as with the larger asters.

All asters are excellent for indoor arrangements, especially if the stems are plunged into cold water as soon as they are cut.

Cyclamen cultivars come in a bewildering range

with flowers in all shapes and sizes

Cyclamen

Familiar all over the world, the cyclamen is one of the most popular houseplants, yet this extraordinary genus grows wild only in Europe, North Africa and Asia Minor. The vast range of pot varieties all originate from a single species, *C. persicum*, which grows on the rocky terrain of the Eastern Mediterranean, but you have to look quite hard to find obvious similarities between the original species and the huge diversity of domesticated varieties offered for sale.

As well as the pot plants, there is a small but choice number of species which thrive outdoors, even in the frostiest of gardens. Hardiest and easiest of these is *C. hederifolium*, a Northern and Central European wildling which, if happy in dappled shade on free-draining soil, develops huge colonies of mature tubers which may reach more than 30cm (12in) across, and blooms copiously year after year. The first flowers of *C. hederifolium* appear at the end of summer when the nights are just beginning to get chilly. They are naked stemmed, either pink or white, and seldom exceed about 10cm (4in) in height. The leaves come after the first flowers so that by the time winter begins a few blooms remain above the richly marbled foliage. Leaf variation is incredible in this species, and as foliage plants they make almost as lovely a display throughout spring and early summer as they do in flower.

The second most common species for autumn colour is *C. cilicium*, a more delicate plant altogether, with smaller, more subtly marbled foliage and shell-pink flowers on shorter stems than *C. hederifolium,* and with petals more frail and delicate. This plant is less tolerant of sustained frost, and will need a measure of winter protection in a cold garden.

From Greece comes a highly variable species, *C. graecum*, whose flowers are also pink or white but whose foliage can display remarkable patterning. As it is not truly frost hardy it is best raised in an alpine pan under glass.

FROM THE TOP:

The small, pink, fragrant blooms of C. africanum *emerge before the foliage.*

Known as 'sowbread' because, according to some, pigs were said to enjoy uprooting the loaf-like tubers, C. hederifolium *is a Northern and Central European wildling.*

The sweptback petals of C. intaminatum *are marked with pencil-fine lines.*

RIGHT: *The intensely fragrant flowers of this* C. persicum *cultivar have long, thin sweptback petals. Colours may be soft pink, carmine or white and usually have darker centres. The leaves have silvery or grey marbling.*

LIRIOPE MUSCARI

A durable character is *Liriope muscari*, with leathery, strap-shaped leaves which do little all summer other than provide a dark background or foil to the brighter summer subjects. But in autumn, a generous clump of purple flower spikes appears which lasts through to the frost. Each individual flower is like a small purple pearl. These plants seem not to care a jot where they grow, unless in shade so dense that they are prevented from flowering or in soil so wet that the roots rot. Divide the plants, when you feel like it, to create more plants.

TULBAGHIA VIOLACEA

A close relative of the onion, *Tulbaghia violacea* produces an almost endless succession of flower stems topped with blooms in a unique shade of violet. Neat foliage and a polite spreading habit that is not at all invasive make this African native a first choice garden plant. Do not attempt to pick blooms for indoors, since the leaves and stems smell unpleasantly like rotting rubber into which garlic has been rubbed.

SEDUM TELEPHIUM

Whether in leaf or flower, *Sedum* is a superb autumn genus which contributes so much, not only to the borders but also to rock gardens, containers and those often overlooked small holes and corners which offer such interesting planting opportunities for species that do not mind growing in poor conditions. *Sedum telephium* is a rather variable species of tall, herbaceous plants whose foliage can often be dark and whose flowers may exhibit an interesting range of colours. Sometimes, these plants will hybridize with other sedum species growing within bee range, to produce some delightful offspring with excellent foliage and bright flowers in colours that vary from creamy green to dusky red or amber.

One of the excitements of autumn are the 'surprise' plants, species which pop up from what looks like bare ground. After the colchicums come the amazing African native *Amaryllis belladonna*, whose bulbs need good summer sunshine in order to ripen sufficiently to produce the flower spikes which are topped with sumptuous pink lily blooms. The leaves follow in spring, and can be untidy unless sited where other plant growth disguises them. These bulbs seem to bloom best when the clumps are so congested that the top ones are being forced out of the ground by others developing beneath them.

Some species of snowdrop share this habit, flowering in autumn without any leaves at what seems to be quite the wrong season. *Galanthus reginae-olgae* and *G. corcyrensis* both hail from Greece, where they grow in drier, more open ground than their late winter-blooming cousins. Certain true crocuses, including *Crocus sativus*, from which genuine saffron is extracted, come up naked in autumn, too. The queen of autumn lilies, the nerine, also presents herself unclothed. The hardiest of these is *Nerine bowdenii*, whose wavy pink petals are curled and gently ruffled. There are redder species, such as *N. undulata* which will provide a long season of glorious blooms in a warm, protected frost-free site.

The New World sages, or salvias, make a generous contribution to the autumn garden, especially in a warm sheltered spot in a gentle climate. Mediterranean salvias prefer life tough and dry, but the more tender species need a plentiful supply of moisture at their roots and warm sunshine to stimulate flowering. Among the blues, the hooked blossoms of *Salvia patens* have already flowered, but later comes the tall, shrubby *S. guaranitica*, whose flowers are an intriguing dusky purple blue, and cherry red *S. microphylla neurepia*. Both these plants have a distinctive aroma, but the related *S. rutilans* has foliage which, when crushed, smells exactly like pineapple, a delightful bonus to the showy red flowers.

ABOVE: *The naked stems of* Amaryllis belladonna *'Barbeton' erupt in autumn, rising quickly to almost 45cm (18in) before the clusters of pink hanging flowers appear.*

By now, the season is gathering momentum. Days are noticeably shorter, the air more chill and, in cold regions frost is increasingly likely, not merely a dusting of rime on the foliage, but a full blown air frost. Less hardy herbaceous perennials such as dahlias, pelargoniums and argyranthemums will succumb as soon as air temperatures have dipped below zero, yet despite the loss of these flowers, there is still a great wealth of colour and form in the garden. Indeed, chilly nights actually enhance the performance of some plants, colouring some foliage to deeper hues of red, russet and yellow, prinking out other, more durable leaves with touches of bronze or purple and brightening the tones of evergreens and conifers. Against this background of shifting colour, mid-autumn flowers seem to brighten, to take on a second wind.

As ever, members of the daisy family, especially those herbaceous species from the grasslands of the world, make the greatest contributions. The rudbeckias, in gold, rusty red and yellow tones, are at their best. Tall perennial kinds such as R. 'Goldsturm' and the double-flowered R. 'Goldquelle' will provide warm-coloured flowers for weeks. For a focal point, R. 'Herbstsonne' (syn. R. 'Autumn Sun') grows to around 2.2m (7ft), and sports big, golden blooms with drooping petals. It flops about limply, though, and needs supporting stakes. Rudbeckias respond well to mid-season feeding and flower best when there has been a steady rainfall.

Closely related to rudbeckias, and like them from North America, the heleniums have an even greater elegance of flower. Each bloom has a conical or rounded centre from which the outer rays are swept back. Late in the season, *Helenium autumnale* carries rusty yellow or brown blooms on long stems, and needs staking. Its hybrids and cultivars often grow shorter: 'Bruno' is a gorgeous mahogany red; 'Butterpat' is clean yellow; and 'Wyndley', which grows no more than 70cm (28in), has brownish cones and brilliant yellow petals.

LEFT: *The yellows, browns and brooding maroons of heleniums make a warm contribution to the border. H. 'Moerheim Beauty' is particularly richly coloured.*

RUDBECKIA HIRTA 'Goldilocks'

Besides the more perennial forms of rudbeckia, there are garden forms raised from *R. hirta* which sport even bigger, brighter flowers. Although technically short-lived perennials, these are best raised annually from seed. 'Goldilocks' is a double form with rather bunched orange-yellow flowers, but there are also fine singles in dark brown, orange and tan shades. 'Nutmeg' is a series of semi-double blooms in autumnal tints and 'Green Eyes' has vivid gold to orange single blooms with yellow-green centres.

PHYSALIS ALKEKENGI

The decorative part of the Chinese lantern plant is actually the sheathed fruit. The flowers themselves are small and white with yellow centres, and they come earlier in the year. Their similarity to nightshade, potato and tomato flowers gives away their identity as members of the family Solanaceae. The subspecies *Physalis alkekengi franchetii* is the most commonly grown. Physalis enjoys a warm, sheltered position in fertile soil which does not dry out. As the fruits are poisonous, they should not be confused with the cape gooseberry (*P. peruviana*), an edible species.

RUDBECKIA 'Herbstsonne'

Literally meaning 'Autumn Sun', *Rudbeckia* 'Herbstsonne' is one of the tallest of the group, often exceeding 2m (6ft) in height before the large, golden yellow blooms open. Like all rudbeckias, it has broad outer petals swept back from the conspicuous, cone-shaped centre, which is bright green in young blooms. The stems are inclined to be lax so support is essential.

97

Dendranthemas (chrysanthemums) have been in cultivation so long that their wild forebears are not fully known.

Dendranthema

The recent reclassification by the world's taxonomic botanists of chrysanthemum to dendranthema has caused much confusion among gardeners. For the sake of technical accuracy, we have to call them by their correct name, but British 'chrysanths' or American 'mums' are exactly as they always were.

For practical gardeners in cool climates, the easiest varieties are outdoor kinds, and of these the toughest are probably the so-called Koreans. These are mainly spray dendranthema, such as the garnet-red 'Duchess of Edinburgh' or bronze 'Coppernob'. The 'Mei-kyo' group are extra tough and extra special. 'Mei-kyo' itself originated in Japan and bears a heavy crop of neat, plummy pink button flowers on compact, shrubby plants. From this variety came such new cultivars as 'Bronze Elegance' and the brilliant golden-yellow 'Nantyderry Sunshine'. Groups of garden dendranthema are constantly being added to. From the U.S.A., for example, comes the latest series, Yoder Garden Mums, a group of tough, dwarf, early flowering spray kinds in good clean colours.

Dendranthema culture, especially for competition, has been the subject of many entire books. There are secret tricks of the trade, guarded carefully by expert growers, and much advice among enthusiasts, freely given and taken. To generalize is dangerous, but good cultural practice to ensure a good crop of autumn flowers could be summed up as follows. Keep plants young, raising new ones each year by taking basal cuttings from old stools (rootstocks) under glass in late winter. Grow in full light, in containers under glass until danger of frost has passed. Pinch back rooted cuttings to promote branching. As flower stems develop, pinch out side buds on single-bloom varieties but leave spray kinds to develop naturally. Feed regularly throughout the growing period with high nitrogen in the first weeks but thereafter with high potassium fertilizer. Watch for such pests as red spider mite, aphids and for such disease as mildew.

BELOW: *Cleanness of colour and uniform flower shape make* Dendranthema *'Golden Elegance' an excellent choice of large-flowered intermediate hybrid.*

ABOVE: *'Spoon' dendranthema are so called because their outer rays form spoon-ended tubes. They occur in a full range of colours.*

ABOVE: *Spray dendranthemas such as* D. *'Yellow Rylite' are often easier to use in flower arrangements than the heavy-headed large-flowered hybrids.*

LEFT: Dendranthema *'Keith Luxford', an intermediate, large-flowered hybrid, must have all subordinate buds removed to encourage single show-size blooms.*

ABOVE: *Even before winter has begun, the paperwhite narcissus (*Narcissus papyraceus*),*

brings a welcome breath of spring, fragrancing an entire room as its flowers open.

As autumn creeps towards its darker end, it is pleasant to be reminded that spring is getting nearer, too, as well as winter. Although the main season for enjoying forced bulbs is a week or two after the shortest day, the paperwhite narcissus (*N. papyraceus*) is easy to coax into bloom extra early. Bulbs that have been specially prepared by the bulb merchant will flower within a few weeks of planting. All you need is a water-tight bowl, some gravel and the bulbs. Plant the bulbs in the gravel with their tops just showing, place the bowl in a warm, well-lit spot and keep about 2cm (1in) of water in the bottom of the bowl throughout the bulbs' development. The flower stems will develop so fast you can almost see them move. When the first blooms open, the fragrance will be so strong, you will forget the winter looming outside.

Outdoors, the summer display has totally finished, and as frost threatens any but the toughest of species, most plants go into dormancy. Foliage has fallen or is about to fall, and there is a dishevelled look to beds and borders. A few perennials provide glimpses of final colour. Vernonias and eupatoriums can still look good. *Eupatorium rugosum* is a plant of quiet beauty, having handsome green foliage all summer and producing sprays of pure white, tufty flowers in late autumn. Air frost can damage these, but in flower arrangements, they have a pleasant, airy, summer feel. In addition to sternbergias (see right, below) other bulbs include the autumn-flowering snowflakes (*Leucojum autumnale* and *L. nicaeense*), which have tiny, pink-flushed white bells. They do best in a free-draining soil, preferably sheltered from the worst frosts.

Attractive seed heads help to eke out the floral beauty of the well-planned border. Sawwort is a pretty North American and European genus, so called because the serrated leaves look viciously spiny but are actually soft to the touch. The purple thistle-like blooms are long over but the exhausted seed capsules are as pretty as any flower at this time of year.

JASMINUM NUDIFLORUM

That miracle of Chinese climbers, the winter jasmine, should be producing its first yellow blooms. Even if the flowers are spoilt outdoors by winter weather, the green stems are attractive enough on their own, and will soon be hung with a fresh crop of blossom if picked and brought into the warm. This plant is easy to propagate from cuttings, but it is easier still to find stem ends that have dunked themselves in the ground and taken root. Simply dig these up and replant them.

LONICERA JAPONICA

Although this is really the season for such winter-flowering honeysuckles as *Lonicera fragrantissima* or *L. x purpusii*, certain summer species still carry a last few blooms. In certain climates, Japanese honeysuckle (*L. japonica*) flowers almost perpetually, and even where winters are cold it continues to produce paired blooms along new stems right up to and after the first of the frosts. Neither showy nor especially shapely at this time of year, these final pale yellow blooms are prized for their sweet fragrance. Whenever you venture outside, to select your flower for the day, linger by this honeysuckle and look for a sprig that carries buds.

STERNBERGIA LUTEA

The sternbergias are a refreshing change from all the pinks and mauves of the autumn bulbs such as amaryllis or colchicum. With glossy, dark green leaves and golden flowers, these bulbs have a spring-like appearance that reminds one of early crocuses. They are happiest in mild areas where summers are hot, so elsewhere they need to be mulched generously to provide winter protection from the worst of the frosts.

CAMELLIA 'Donation'

Hardiest of the 'tea trees', *Camellia x williamsii*
has varieties which produce sporadic blooms
throughout the late autumn and winter, ending
with a final flourish at the beginning of spring.
Among the most dependable varieties are those
with single or semi-double pink flowers, of which
'Donation' is the most prolific bloomer. Severe
frost will brown the blooms so if cold weather
is forecast, get busy with the secateurs and
bring open flowers indoors for safety. The plants
themselves are perfectly hardy, provided their roots
are not allowed to freeze right through.

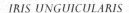

IRIS UNGUICULARIS

The winter-flowering iris performs best in a hot, dry
site. There are several interesting varieties including a
white form known as *Iris unguicularis alba*, a tiny
form known as *I. unguicularis* 'Oxford Dwarf' and
the deep purplish blue 'Mary Barnard'. Although slow
to establish themselves, these plants are not difficult to
grow, but they should be left undisturbed so that they
can slowly expand to form generous flowering clumps.
Division is unnecessary, unless you want to acquire new plants.

SEDUM 'Autumn Joy'

This late-flowering, seed-sterile form of the ice plant,
has darker, redder blooms than the more frequently
grown *Sedum spectabile*. It is lovely in the company
of the lighter-flowered *S. spectabile* 'Brilliant' and the
related *S. telephium*. The flowers are attractive to
butterflies hungry for a last feed to build up their
energy reserves for hibernation. Although perfectly happy
if left alone, sedums grow better if divided every three

years so that their stems remain young and sturdy. Failure to divide the plants will result in
lax stems which could collapse in rough weather.

As the shortest day approaches, autumn concludes its final
display and leads into winter. Garden beauty has to be sought
with a little more diligence than at other times. The last few
roses fade with the closing of the season. Some groups,
especially the rugosas, the Chinas and the hybrid musks, will
have provided a glorious autumn display, often carrying
flowers and hips together, making for some interesting colour
contrasts. The hybrid musks, a group developed early this
century by an English clergymen, the Rev. Joseph Pemberton,
are especially good at producing an autumn flush, and even
though their last flowers may be caught by frost their beauty
carries on right up to winter's threshold.

At the front of the mixed border, summer sedums refuse
to give up. Even though their flowers are long over, the
outline of those flat-topped stems present much character,
and their colours, still suffused with russet and purple, persist
until highlighted a final time with a sugar coating of hoar
frost. As well as looking lovely, the dying flower heads of
these plants are havens for small insects and are, therefore,
much visited by tiny songbirds made hungry by the
increasingly cold weather.

Among new arrivals, the late autumn brings the first, or,
if you prefer, the last of the irises, particularly the
Mediterranean species, *I. unguicularis* (see left, centre).
Nothing could be fresher than these delicate blue blooms
appearing among the winter-roughened, straw-like foliage.
They are vulnerable to wind damage, however, and are best
enjoyed when picked and taken indoors rather than left to the
weather. Although completely hardy, these plants resent being
moved, and will often sulk for one or even two whole seasons
if they are transplanted before settling down to flower each
autumn and winter. They are happy, however, in the poorest
and driest of soils and seem to do best at the very base of a
hot dry wall, even if their roots are buried in building rubble.

RIGHT: *Touched by frost,* Rosa *'Felicia', a musk rose which flowers from early
summer, retains its beauty until the sun melts the crystals and browns the petals.*

When gorgeous flowers are few and far between,

catkins link winter with spring

Catkins

Catkins may not be obvious as flowers, but many of them are fascinating to watch as they open on mild days, and most have great beauty. *Garrya elliptica* (see page 106) probably picks up the prize for its catkins, being so well set among the evergreen foliage. When they are still in tight bud, they are presented at the ends of the twigs, in assorted clusters, their scaly leaves overlapping. As they open to produce pollen, they achieve surprising lengths, several centimetres in some cases, and hang perfectly straight, making a pleasing contrast with the waved leaves.

Hazel nuts (*Corylus avellana*) have pretty catkins, too, especially the contorted form whose mature male flowers, like those of *Garrya*, hang perfectly straight, making a disciplined contrast with the curiously tortuous stems. Look carefully among the twigs to find the female nut flowers, usually lower down the stems, forming tiny red tufts of stigmas which await the wind-blown pollen.

Alder (*Alnus glutinosa*) can sometimes be mistaken for hazel, since its male tassels are very hazel-like, but the female flowers, which resemble tiny fir cones, are produced on the same tree and are unmistakable. Alder trees grow large quite quickly and so need thoughtful siting, but where there is plenty of space they are a beautiful genus, making a fine summer background for other plants and acting as windbreaks for more vulnerable species.

The most strokeable catkins of all grow on the willows. These, like kittens, (the words have the same derivation) have a furry appeal and can gleam like silver in the sunlight. Look for *Salix daphnoides* and *S. acutifolia*, whose stems are covered with bluish or white blooms, as well as the more showy goat willow (*S. caprea*) and its close Chinese relative *S. hookeriana*. The low-growing *S. gracilistyla* 'Melanostachys' has jet-black furry catkins, and the oddity *S. udensis* (syn. *S. sacchalinensis*) is beloved of flower arrangers. The fasciated stems of *S. udensis* 'Sekka' are crushed and fused into flat, twisted shapes. A grotesque plant but one of interest in the winter garden.

ABOVE: *The hanging male tassels and female cone-like flowers of alder (*Alnus glutinosa*) create an attractive outline on naked stems.*

BELOW: *Hanging straight down, the catkins of the contorted hazel (*Corylus avellana* 'Contorta') stand out against its tortuous stems.*

ABOVE: *The flowers of the goat or pussy willow (*Salix caprea*) remain furry through winter, but will not open before early spring.*

RIGHT: *The silky grey catkins of the willow* Salix irrorata *open to reveal yellow anthers. This deciduous shrub is further enhanced by a pale dusty bloom that covers its young stems and shoots.*

ABOVE: *Male, catkin-like flowers of the North American evergreen shrub* Garrya elliptica

begin to extend when the weather gets colder and last for most of the winter.

At the very end of the growing season, as the shortest days approach, flowers are harder to find. In cold regions rare blooms such as a late rose or an early primula are often damaged by frost or even covered by early falls of snow.

Wall plants, especially on sheltered sites, still provide interest. *Garrya elliptica* (see left), the evergreen North American native, makes an excellent wall shrub, acting as a good-natured host, perhaps, for herbaceous climbers in summer but then developing its grey-green catkins to take autumn into winter. There are male and female plants but the males have the longest catkins, hanging straight as pokers among the green, eggshell-textured foliage.

To flower well, and to keep to the contours of the wall, *Garrya elliptica* must be pruned, preferably in late winter or early spring, to give new growths time to mature and form flower buds. Any old or dead wood should be removed when this becomes most apparent, usually just before the new leaves begin to emerge. If you want extra long stems for cutting purposes allow some of the twigs to grow unhindered and unclipped, but tie them loosely to the wall to prevent the plant from looking untidy. Similar techniques work with such other autumn- and winter-flowering wall plants as wintersweet (see page 116) and Japanese quince (see page 119), whose fruits will have ripened by now and can be harvested for making into delicious jelly.

So the season concludes and the year moves towards its quietest period. Now is the time to take careful stock, to note any deficiencies in your planting and to select for an improved collection. Be sure to include those very special varieties that provide colour and interest when daylight is at a premium and when venturing outdoors needs strong motivation. With careful planning, you should be able to gather a flower to enjoy every day of the year, even during autumn and winter, no matter how harsh the climate.

SENECIO x HYBRIDUS 'Cindi'

In the wild cinerarias, or more correctly *Senecio*, have mauve to pink blooms, but garden forms can be almost any shade of blue, white, purple, or be bi-coloured. Pot-grown cinerarias are short-day plants, bringing masses of clean, vivid colours to the autumn and winter conservatory collection. Easy to grow from seed, most modern seed series are of small or medium-sized plants. Cinerarias are best kept reasonably cool all summer and protected from strong, direct sunlight. They are hungry feeders, demanding a weekly liquid manure solution and a gentle increase in heat as they come into bloom. As they are prone to aphid attack, biological aphid control or regular treatments with aphicides are essential.

EUCHARIS AMAZONICA

Eucharis amazonica (syn. *E. grandiflora*), a richly fragrant member of the daffodil family, comes from the Amazon rain forests. The white flowers are exactly narcissus-shaped, and are borne in umbels carrying as many as six or seven blooms per main stem. These bulbs require humidity of at least 50 per cent and humus-rich, lime-free soil as  similar in quality to the dense layers of leaves, in varying stages of decomposition, which litter the rain-forest floor. To achieve a long run of flowers, plant bulbs in succession through spring and summer in a conservatory or heated greenhouse.

CORTADERIA SELLOANA 'Pumila'

Planted in a wise position, the so-called pampas grasses can be focal points of immense beauty. The South American *Cortaderia selloana* produces huge silvery creamy inflorescences in autumn which persist into winter. More compact that most, the form 'Pumila' is capable of reaching 1.8m (6ft), with flowers held proudly above the foliage.  Although vigorous and robust, proving almost indestructible when mature, pampas grasses can be tricky to establish. Divisions are best made in spring, replanting just before growth begins. In late winter, if it is safe to do so, the old growths can be burnt off. If you plan to cut the plant back, do be careful: rubbed the wrong way, the leaves are razor sharp.

ABOVE: *The flowers of* Chaenomeles speciosa *cannot survive a coating of hoar frost.*

Fortunately, new blooms will soon replace them.

Flowers are harder to find during the shortest days than at any other time of the year, but that gives each discovery more value

Winter

Floral beauty may be harder to find in winter than during the main growing season, but seek and you cannot fail to find. You will need strong motivation to venture outdoors, especially in cold weather, but making the effort can surprise you with rich rewards: the first snowdrops, a last remaining rose restored to beauty by a coating of frost crystals or, perhaps, an early glimpse of that queen of winter flowers, the hellebore. And when picked and brought indoors for closer contemplation, a twig of wintersweet or a camellia bud closed tightly against the weather can give as much pleasure as a vast colourful bouquet of summer roses.

RIGHT: *The pink-flushed white flowers of Chaenomeles speciosa 'Moerloosei' first appear on naked stems.*

FAR RIGHT: *When forced in the greenhouse Hippeastrum 'Apple Blossom' produces spectacular flowers to be enjoyed during winter's darkest months.*

Winter has its own special abundance — and not just of snow and ice. Each flower goes further, standing out among the browns and duns

Winter beauty

Flowers are scarcest at the beginning of the official winter — the shortest day, or winter solstice — but as soon as the days begin discernibly to lengthen, plant hormones are stimulated and the whole process of starting up another season lumbers slowly into motion. In cold

continental climates, the dormancy period can last right through the season, and changes in plant life are hard to detect. Wherever there is a maritime influence, though, particularly where oceans bring warm currents, growth will begin. This will be hesitant at first, perhaps proceeding for only an hour or two at midday when there is sun. By late winter a huge variety of bulbs, shrubs and trees will be coming rapidly into flower. Such early blooming plants risk losing all to night frost, however. Fortunately, most have plenty of blooms in reserve, enabling them to provide a long run of colour between cold snaps. To ensure an abundance of blooms through winter requires sound planning, and it may be necessary to arrange for protection from the worst of the climate, even in areas where seasons are mild. Temporary windbreaks are helpful. More lasting protection is easy to achieve by careful placing

of well-anchored screen plants around the garden's boundary.

A hedge is the most obvious choice for a natural windbreak, but strategic placing of trees and shrubs, especially in line with the prevailing winds, can be almost as effective and will create interesting focal points. Many windbreak plants can be selected to look their best in winter, whether in flower or in fruit. Evergreen *Viburnum tinus* (see page 112), for example, is an excellent dense shrub for fighting off gales, and produces a generous show of winter flowers that are pink in the bud opening to pure white. Hollies make effective shelter, too, and provide cover for wildlife as well as making an interesting background.

As frost or wind can damage frail blooms, it is is a good idea to

carry secateurs during garden strolls, ready for culling flowers while they are still in bud. In warmth, branches of forsythia, winter jasmine, wintersweet and even the mid-spring-flowering *Ribes sanguineum* will rush into flower within a few days of being picked

provided you first crush the stems then change their water at least every second day. More delicate plants, such as schizostylis or the fragile blue *Iris unguicularis*, actually prefer life indoors, producing perfect blooms untouched by frost. Outdoors, their lives are brief and violent.

It is indoors that winter blooms can be the most spectacular. Potted cyclamen, spring bulbs brought on early, the first mimosa under glass, and the exquisite fragrance that goes with it, these are the particular treats of winter gardening. In cold climates the quest for a daily bloom is made so much easier if you are lucky enough to own a conservatory or greenhouse. Constant supplies of huge blooms can be had from such obliging plants as perpetual carnations or certain varieties of indoor roses. Special to the season are the large, showy cyclamen and indoor primulas such as *Primula obconica* and *P. malacoides*.

LEFT: *The beautiful early flowers of* Primula whitei *make this plant well worth growing.*

ABOVE: Cornus mas *produces tiny blooms.* ABOVE RIGHT: Crocus tommasinianus.

VIBURNUM TINUS 'Eve Price'

One of the most valuable evergreen shrubs, Viburnum tinus blooms in winter as well as producing flowers sporadically all year, and sometimes carries blue-black berries. The species itself is of great value, but the compact cultivar V. tinus 'Eve Price' is especially useful in a small space. The shrub looks best just before the main late winter flush of flowers, when half the blossom is still in tight bud making a rosy contrast with the white of the open blooms. Pruning is unnecessary. Any soil will do, even if dry and chalky, and there is no need to feed such a tough plant once it is well established.

LEUCOJUM VERNUM

In its wild European habitat, the spring snowflake will penetrate a covering of snow to flower above it. Soon after the shortest day, the first tiny white blooms begin to thrust above the folded, deep green leaf tips. Each bloom is soon fully open, while the stems are still only a couple of centimetres high. As winter progresses, the stems lengthen and the flowers enlarge, developing a green band around their pleated rims. These bulbs are happiest grown in shade, in soil that does not dry out too much in summer. Divide congested clumps as for snowdrops (see page 120).

HYACINTHUS ORIENTALIS 'Distinction'

When little else is flowering, large, specially treated Hyacinthus orientalis bulbs provide startling colour and heady fragrance indoors. 'Distinction' is just one of the dozens of cultivars available offering colours which run through all the blues, pale and dark pink, purple, white and cream. Plant the bulbs in bowls at the end of summer and submerge these in cold compost, peat or ashes. Either place them outside or keep cold and dark indoors. When the shoots reach 2.5cm (1in) in height, usually around a month after planting, bring the bowls gradually into the light, but delay their entry into the full heat of the living room until the flowers have begun to open.

How remarkable is the heather family. Not only is it abundant throughout the temperate world (southern Africa alone boasts more than 600 wild species) but it also has the goodness, through one species or another, to provide flowers at almost any time of year. For winter colour, the two species *Erica carnea* and *E. erigena* along with the hybrid *E.* x *darleyensis* are best. Such varieties as *E. carnea* 'Springwood Pink' (see right) will flower for many months; it will also form weed-proof mats of pleasant summer foliage if grouped together. In any natural heather garden, such summer-flowering species as *E. vagans* look well in winter too, not only for the greenness of their foliage, but also for the quiet beauty of their spent blooms. Although these may have turned brown or russet, they will have kept their shape and texture.

The great majority of heathers prefer sandy or peaty, lime-free soil. However, some winter-flowering types, especially *E.* x *darleyensis*, are relatively lime tolerant, particularly when grown in a free-draining soil into which plenty of organic matter has been worked. Little pruning is needed, although the plants will stay more compact if they are trimmed over once a year, when flowering is nearly done; imagine the action of a grazing sheep and imitate that.

Under glass, apart from a little early seed sowing, this is a relatively quiet period, with little to do but enjoy the blooming of indoor primulas, early bulbs and cyclamen. *Primula obconica* makes an especially fine display in the white, mauve, pink and blue colour range. As some skins are allergic to its foliage, it should be handled as little as possible.

Hyacinths and narcissus which have been specially prepared by the bulb merchant for forcing can be coaxed into flower around the shortest day of the year, or even before to provide an abundance of indoor colour and fragrance several months before their natural flowering season outdoors (see *Hyacinthus orientalis* 'Distinction', left).

ABOVE: *Winter blooming and lime tolerant,* Erica carnea *'Springwood Pink' is one of the*

heather species useful for providing mats of colour over the winter months.

The few weeks that follow the winter solstice are the most challenging for flower hunters, particularly outdoors, when even such long-term performers as Japanese honeysuckle and late asters begin to falter. The last of the dendranthemas (chrysanthemums) may still show colour, especially if frosts have not been too severe. *Dendranthema* 'Emperor of China', grown by the Chinese hundreds, if not thousands of years ago, reaches more than 1.5m (4ft), has lax growth and not very large, ragged, double flowers, but the silvery pink of the petals contrasts delightfully with the foliage, which turns beetroot red as it ages in early winter.

The stinking iris (*I. foetidissima*) is a modest summer bloom that becomes conspicuous in winter when its extraordinary seed capsules open. These curl back on themselves, revealing rows of vivid orange seed that are flower-like from the distance, adding flashes of bright colour to the winter scene (see right top). Given the right conditions, winter pansies (see left) will produce a steady, although somewhat sporadic run of cheerful blooms, and are especially useful for containers and borders.

Help also comes now from fragrant viburnums such as white-flowered *Viburnum farreri* and the larger-flowered pink *V.* x *bodnantense* (see page 119). During mild spells from autumn to spring, winter cherry (*Prunus subhirtella* 'Autumnalis') (see page 119) breaks out in a profusion of pink or white blooms. Although easily damaged by air frost, these last well in cold and damp.

Indoors, such modern hybrid cyclamen as the oddly named *Cyclamen* 'Turbo Laser' series will flower within nine months of sowing. For more traditional beauty, sweet-scented forms of *C. persicum* have leaner, more shapely flowers, usually pale pink or white with pink eyes (see also page 92). Watch out for vine weevil, which could blight your winter display but which can be controlled with biological methods.

LEFT: *Winter pansies (*Viola *Universal Series), the most popular of pansies come in a broad range of colours, both plain and two-tone.*

IRIS FOETIDISSIMA

As each seed capsule of the stinking iris ripens and dries, it ruptures and folds back to form a triple bed on which the bright orange seeds lie, contrasting with the parchment colour of the dried, everted pods. *I. foetidissima* prefers dry, chalky conditions in semi-shade. Established plants flower best as this is one of those unusual perennials that actually prefer not to be divided. To increase stocks, collect a few seeds, sow them in moist compost in shade, and plant out the resulting young plants a year later.

ARBUTUS UNEDO

At this time of year, a mature specimen of the small strawberry tree could surprise you with flowers shaped like tiny paper lanterns, often accompanying the previous year's crop of rough-skinned, orange-red fruit that give this plant its colloquial name. Growing naturally in mild, high-rainfall climates, *Arbutus unedo* prefers rich, peaty soil which retains some of its moisture in summer. Sustained, heavy frost can damage the top growth, but even if cut to the ground, new shoots will usually appear from the roots as soon as spring comes. If this happens, saw off the old, dead portions of the plant but wait until you are absolutely sure that they are dead before you take that irrevocable step.

CITRUS SINENSIS

In warm climates, orange and lemon blossom scent hangs heavy on the air throughout the latter half of winter. In cold regions, where such tender plants as this *Citrus sinensis* can be grown under glass, blossoms will often open in midwinter, fragrancing whole rooms with a single flower. Quietly beautiful, but particularly attractive when seen on the evergreen bushes accompanied by the previous year's ripened fruits, citrus blossom is waxy white or off-white, and forms clusters with several flowers opening at a time over long periods. Although easy to grow, most members of the orange and lemon family prefer lime-free compost. Young plants develop surprisingly quickly during the growing season and therefore need regular feeding, especially when grown in containers.

115

HEDERA HELIX

The ivies are such a useful group for foliage that few gardeners appreciate the quiet beauty of their flowers. Most species have two kinds of growth: juvenile and adult. Like young children, juvenile ivies delight in running about, climbing and clinging to supporting objects, whereas the adult is more shrubby in growth and stands out from the support plant (or fence or wall). The pale yellowish green flowers appear in clusters and have small stamens and petals. If humans overlook them, the bees and butterflies certainly do not, and feast on the rich supply of nectar that they provide. Through winter, the flowers gradually, almost imperceptibly transform into clusters of dark berries.

HELLEBORUS NIGER 'Potter's Wheel'

Planted out, a mixed batch of *Helleborus niger* seedlings will produce a fine display. But if space is limited, a cultivar or seedling selection that stands head and shoulders above the rest is required. The seed series *H.niger* 'Potter's Wheel', raised in the 1950s by the famous English specialist Hilda Davenport Jones, boasts large, exceptionally well-

formed, pure white blooms, which are produced in profusion in late winter. Seedlings raised from this series will come relatively true, but exercise ruthless selection, weeding out and discarding all but the very finest progeny. A lover of rich, cool soil that does not bake too dry in summer, *H. niger* will thank you for an occasional summer soaking, especially during a drought, by providing a greater number of winter blooms.

MAHONIA JAPONICA

This is the only member of the spiny, largely evergreen genus of shrubs whose flowers are truly fragrant. During summer buds form at the tips of the stems then extend in winter to produce a bunch of flowering stems, each arranged in a shallow 'S' shape and hung with tiny, primrose-yellow blooms. The scent is almost identical to that of lily of the valley (see page 30). Leggy shrubs can be cut hard back to the ground to stimulate the production of new stems. Push the cut stems deep into good, moist soil to make new plants.

Winter shrubs often carry the sweetest fragrances. The papery blooms of the wintersweets (*Chimonanthus*), which originate from China, fill the air with a luscious scent through much of the season. The straw-coloured blooms have purple centres. Appearing on twiggy growths, they look more like their stylized portraits in old Chinese silk paintings than do any other flowers, apart, perhaps, from the Japanese quinces (*Chaenomeles*) (see page 119).

In cold gardens, wintersweets are happiest grown against a warm wall facing towards the sun. *Chimonanthus praecox* can be reluctant to bloom in its first few seasons and is best left unpruned until a year or two after the first successful flowering of starry, parchment-and-purple blooms. This might take up to seven years, but is well worth the wait. Thereafter, prune gently every year after flowering to encourage the plant to grow more flowering spurs. The resulting abundance of short stems should all develop several flower buds ready to flower the following year.

Even though spring is months away yet, the pluckiest of the spring plants will produce an occasional sporting bloom. Primroses, for instance, sometimes flower throughout winter (see page 135). *Primula vulgaris sibthorpii*, a subspecies from Asia Minor, does this readily. Beloved of Jacobean gardeners in the early part of the seventeenth century, this gentle lavender-coloured plant was the one that introduced a pink or purple gene to the European primrose family.

When it is cold outdoors and you would like more than a chilled, frost-pocked flower or two to enjoy, why not dig up an entire primrose plant from the garden, disturbing the roots as little as possible, and plant it in a roomy pot. Placed in a greenhouse or conservatory or on a well-lit windowsill, the resulting flowers can be enjoyed at close quarters, and having the plant indoors will also enable their faint but sweetly pervasive fragrance to be savoured.

RIGHT: *Wintersweet* (Chimonanthus praecox) *produces its intensely fragrant blooms soon after the shortest day, and continues to flower for the rest of winter.*

ABOVE: *Like most of the Japanese quinces,* Chaenomeles speciosa *'Moerloosei' will venture a*

flower or two at the coldest time of year. Any flowers spoilt by frost will be replaced.

Winter aconites (*Eranthis hyemalis*) should be racing into bloom by now, especially if there is a sunny spell. They are particularly lovely under trees, where they blend with grasses or the foliage of other shade-loving plants and reflect the slanting rays of the sun. In good border soil, the aconites' larger cousins, the florist's anemones (*Anemone coronaria*) will provide a bloom or two for cutting (see page 127). The double 'Saint Brigid' has more petals but the single 'De Caen' comes out top for perfection of flower shape, and the silver-ringed black centres look good on the red or scarlet varieties.

Branches of the Japanese quinces (*Chaenomeles japonica*, *C. speciosa* and *C. x superba*) open well when taken indoors, but by this stage in winter they should be showing several blooms in full colour outside. Most Japanese quinces have blossom in the red, salmon or coral range, but *C. speciosa* 'Moerloosei' opens greenish white soon to become flushed, like apple blossom, with pink. *C. x superba* 'Nivalis' is a clean white and *C. x superba* 'Pink Lady' a clear, shell pink. To maximize their beauty, *Chaenomeles* are best grown on a wall. Heat reflected from the brick or stonework, even on a chilly wall facing away from the afternoon sun, encourages the first blooms, ensuring a run of flower over several months. Young growths need to be pruned back in late spring to encourage the development of short flowering spurs which should be full of blossom the following winter and spring.

Fragrant indoor winter plants include *Jasminum primulinum*, which should flower over a very long period, and freesias, which make fine midwinter container subjects whether cut for floral arrangement or brought indoors as they grow and flower. Freesia corms can be planted almost at any time of the year, but for winter blooms they should be planted in very free-draining compost in mid- to late summer, outdoors, and brought into protection and gentle heat in cold climates well before there is danger of a frost.

VIBURNUM x BODNANTENSE

Named after Bodnant, the Welsh garden where it was raised, *Viburnum x bodnantense* produces generous clusters of rich pink blooms and a pleasant, though somewhat heavy fragrance. One of its parents, *V. farreri* has smaller clusters of white flowers but is more subtle in its display and sweeter in fragrance. Unlike its bolder, coarser offspring its flowers are inclined to drop when picked, though. Blooming of *V. x bodnantense* begins on old wood, in early winter, but often, newer, larger blooms are formed on the stem tips, just before the foliage emerges for spring. Any soil suits this shrub, even shallow chalk, and it needs little attention other than a severe pruning every seven years or so simply to rejuvenate it. This is one of the easiest plants to propagate by layering or by taking soft cuttings in midsummer or semi-ripe ones in early autumn.

TULIPA HUMILIS PULCHELLA Violacea Group

Among the first of the species tulips to flower, this tiny gem bears little resemblance to the stately plants that will grace a spring border. Seldom reaching more than 13cm (5in), the flowers appear flat on the ground at first then gradually straighten up as the days warm. Their colour is a unique rosy violet. Free-draining soil and full sun are essential and even then the plant will multiply only if it likes the soil.

PRUNUS x SUBHIRTELLA
'Autumnalis Rosea'

A freak clone among spring-flowering cherries, this small tree produces pink blossom (there is also a white form) from mid-autumn until the leaves emerge in spring. It is excellent as a lawn specimen or at the back of a border. As cherries are prone to infection, avoid pruning unless absolutely necessary.

119

*Even after being frozen solid overnight, snowdrops
perk up as soon as the ice in the stems melts*

Snowdrops

To an unpractised eye, all snowdrops (*Galanthus*) look alike. Once you begin to scrutinize the blooms, however, and to look carefully at the different foliage of all the species and subspecies, their diversity will amaze and delight you.

Within the three main groups of snowdrop, there are some wonderful garden examples. *Galanthus plicatus* carries its flowers among broad, outwardly curled foliage. The common snowdrop (*G. nivalis*) comes in literally hundreds of different forms and subspecies from the odd-coloured *G. nivalis lutescens* to the extraordinary autumn snowdrop (*G. reginae-olgae*), a subspecies from Greece whose flowers emerge without foliage in autumn. There are giant snowdrops, like *G.* 'S. Arnott', whose mature bulbs always throw up two blooms, the first of which may be 2.5cm (1in) long, and those like *G.* 'Merlin', with more than their fair share of green markings which make their centres dark and distinctive. Odder forms include *G.* 'Magnet', where the flower pedicels are long and bowed, like a horseshoe magnet, and *G.* 'Scharlockii' whose sepals have processed themselves into pricked rabbit ears. 'Scharlockii' also carries distinctive green tips to its outer petals.

Double-flowered snowdrops have an extraordinary variety of forms. Two distinctive varieties are *G.* 'Ophelia', whose central petals form a neat green-and-white rosette surrounded by symmetrical outer petals, and *G.* 'Lady Beatrix Stanley', a slightly more dishevelled flower with extra petals at the centre.

The doubles tend not to set seed, but single snowdrops are almost all fertile and will produce progeny surprisingly quickly. The named forms do not produce identical offspring, however, so if you wish to keep your stocks pure you will need to multiply by division. All snowdrops should be lifted and divided every few years, as soon as the clumps become congested. Dig up an entire clump, deeply to avoid slicing through the white underground stems. Replant the individual bulbs deep enough to cover all the white part of the stem and 2.5cm (1in) of the green.

BELOW: *The outer petals of* Galanthus nivalis *'Viridipicis', a distinctive form of the common snowdrop, are touched with green.*

BELOW: *In the hybrid* Galanthus *'John Gray' the green central markings are enlarged and suffused through the inner petals.*

BOTTOM: *Green and white stripes at the centres of* G. *'Greatorex Double' blooms are arranged in the shape of rosettes.*

RIGHT: *The common snowdrop* (G. nivalis) *is spectacular enough, but enlarged forms such as* G. *'Atkinsii' make an even more dramatic display.*

ABOVE: Iris reticulata *'Cantab' is just one of many short-stemmed iris varieties that are useful for providing jewel-like colour during gloomy winter months.*

There are stirrings in the garden. Days are still short and temperatures still very low, especially during the night, but the rate at which the nights are receding is on the increase. Small fragment of comfort that may be, but it is enough to spark off an eruption of little bulbs into flower. The bulbous irises, crocuses, early tulips, and even a daffodil or two, are beginning to show colour.

Low-growing reticulata irises (see right, top), look wonderful growing under winter-flowering shrubs such as *Hamamelis japonica* (see right, centre) in a mixed border, their blue flowers contrasting with the warm shades. Later, the broad foliage will throw shade, so it is important for the bulbs to be planted on the sunny side to allow the sun to mature their newly grown corms after flowering.

Petasites fragrans, an invasive monster of a plant unless you have space for it, is throwing up grubby lavender flowers which scent the air with the cherry pie fragrance that one associates with the purple summer flowers of heliotrope, hence the plant's colloquial name, winter heliotrope. Do not be bewitched by these blooms, unless you have a whole paddock or a very rough corner to accommodate the plant, for after the flowers have died, the root stock sets to work forming an impenetrable network that can advance several metres in a season, smothering everything in its path.

In a wild garden or among alpines in the rock garden, *Cyclamen coum*, quite the toughest of the wild cyclamen, produces cerise or carmine buds that look like miniature ship's propellers as they open. Planted among autumn-flowering wild cyclamen (see page 62), their silver-and-green marbled leaves, every one a little different like human finger prints, harmonize. *Cyclamen coum* prefers shade, but has no qualms about getting too dry in summer so does well planted below deciduous trees, even if these are so thirsty that they dry the ground out immediately below their roots.

IRIS RETICULATA 'Katharine Hodgkin'

The black-dotted, navy blue-and orange-blooms of *I. reticulata* are generously sized and on stems short enough to avoid their being blown over by winter gales. These bulbs make excellent subjects for growing in an alpine pan, under cool glass. Varieties of especial note include 'JS Dijt', which is deep reddish purple with yellow eyes; 'Cantab' (see left); and the uniquely coloured 'Katharine Hodgkin', whose dusky Cambridge blue-and-leopard tones are ravishing. 'Reticulata' refers to the net-like casing of the bulb or corm which resembles the *reticulum* (net) used by Roman gladiators. The bulbs or corms need to be planted in a sunny position.

HAMAMELIS JAPONICA

The spreading, naked branches of Japanese witch hazel bloom any time from midwinter onwards. The crinkled yellow flowers, which look like hundreds of little spiders, are one of the delights of the winter garden. Their fragrance has clinical connotations for many since embrocations and anti-inflamatory lotions often contain oil of witch hazel. Neutral or acid soil, into which organic matter has been worked, is preferred, but most hamamelis are moderately lime tolerant.

STACHYURIS PRAECOX

With long catkin-like flowers, *Stachyuris praecox* is a distintive shrub. It is happiest in cool, moist conditions, where the flowers last for a considerable part of winter and spring, and makes a pleasing contrast with evergreens, especially camellias whose glossy foliage provides a useful backdrop to the yellow or beige flowers of the stachyuris.

123

CLIVIA MINIATA

Originating from South Africa's Drakensberg mountains, clivias thrive where trees and rocks create cool, shady corners. Their dark, almost blackish green foliage makes a fine background for the big showy umbels of warm apricot-orange flowers. Flowering continues over several weeks, after which the fruits ripen and turn red. Clivias make superb conservatory subjects and flower best when they have become potbound. They need feeding with high potash fertilizer during the growing period, but should not be replanted until the roots threaten to crack the sides of the pot. Clivias are easy to raise from seed or by dividing mature plants.

HAMAMELIS MOLLIS 'Magic Fire'

With spidery, bright yellow winter flowers on naked stems and superb autumn foliage, Chinese witch hazel is one of the prettiest members of the genus. The deliciously fragrant blooms have interestingly crinkled petals. If protected from the extremes of drought by using thick mulches and watering when necessary, *H. mollis* and its cultivars will reward, in even the most alkaline of gardens, with a fragrant winter display.

LACHENALIA ALOIDES

Homesick settlers of the Cape of Good Hope named the Cape cowslip because its hanging blooms reminded them of the meadow primulas of Europe. It is among the first of the bulbous plants to emerge in southern Africa, but will not survive outdoors in cold regions. It does make a delightful pan subject for an alpine house or gently heated greenhouse, however. Bulbs can be divided and replanted before they become congested, but need to be handled with care since bruised bulbs can rot. If you suspect bulb damage, dust with flowers of sulphur to reduce the risk of rotting.

124

One of the most dramatic plants from the eastern side of southern Africa, *Clivia miniata* (see left, top) has deep green strap-like leaves and soft apricot-orange flowers which last for many weeks. Popular all over the warm world as a shade-loving ground cover, in colder regions, where it would not survive outdoors, it makes a ravishing conservatory winter plant. Easy to raise from seed, collected when the 'berries' turn red on the parent plants, clivias must have shade. In the wild, they grow in rocky conditions beneath the forest canopy so a shaded drawing room window or conservatory are equally suitable. In containers, the plants flower best if allowed to become almost pot bound.

Much more delicate in appearance and still in need of winter protection, *Cyclamen libanoticum*, a Middle-Eastern plant that grows close to the last surviving cedars of Lebanon, is exquisite in an alpine pan. The broad, sweptback flowers are an exquisite shade of pale lilac pink, deepening to a cerise or carmine centre. These plants are easy to raise from seed, and the corms need very gritty, free-draining compost and a dry, cool but frost-free habitat.

Outdoors, a little more colour is creeping into the garden each day. Euphorbias, especially *Euphorbia robbiae* and *E. characias* are coming into bloom with bluntly rounded yellow-green spikes. Look out for seedlings of these plants, allowing them to grow in situ if you approve of where they have placed themselves, or carefully replanting if you can think of somewhere better for them. Such tough perennials will not object to being moved so early in the year as long as you do not spoil the structure of the soil as you replant them.

Rosemary is in flower now, too soon to tempt an early bee, perhaps, but pretty enough to pick a sprig and enjoy the gingery aroma. If pruned in late winter, rosemary produces strong new shoots. Do not cut back too hard in case the stress kills the bush, and do not prune during hard weather.

ABOVE: *'Whitewell Purple' is an improved form of the wild species* Crocus tommasinianus, *and has darker purple flowers. It grows best in short turf or at the bases of shrubs.*

Magnolia time is almost here. Already the smaller-flowered kinds are beginning to slough the velvet-coated scale leaves from the flower buds, ready to explode into clouds of white or pink petals as soon as the air warms a little. *M. stellata* often opens too early, getting caught by frost, but usually has a reserve display held safely in bud for a while longer. Quite the easiest cultivar of the hybrid *M. x loebneri* is 'Leonard Messel' (see below) which has lilac-pink buds opening to blush white. Petals in the young flowers appear like leaves in a book, crowded one behind

Magnolia x loebneri *'Leonard Messel' is*

one of the earliest of the magnolias to bloom.

another. Later-flowering magnolias will bloom in spring and summer. All magnolias have fragile root systems and may take a year or two to establish, but these early flowering species are the easiest to grow, and are fully lime tolerant. After the first couple of seasons, resist feeding the plants, since, if they grow too quickly, they will take longer to come into flower.

Japanese apricot (*Prunus mume*) is covered with small pink or white flowers now. Finest of the cultivars is the coral-pink 'Beni-chidore', which grows into a small, well-rounded tree. The flowers have a sweet almond scent. No pruning or training is necessary. Although the plant shrugs off cold, it dislikes an exposed or windy spot.

Such lovely winter-flowering trees as magnolia and prunus look even better when they are planted with carefully chosen ground cover at their feet. The plain, green-leaved lungwort *Pulmonaria rubra* makes a fine companion for *M. stellata*, for example, its tubular coppery-pink flowers blending well with the magnolia's white blooms. To accompany the coral pink blossom of the Japanese apricot, the deep blue flowers and darker leaves of *Pulmonaria angustifolia* might look better. Both of these clump-forming lungworts are easy to grow if kept moist and partly shaded in summer. They should be divided at least every four years, in spring or autumn, to keep them young.

The stippled foliage of the lungworts makes a handsome foil for the first of the anemones. Florist's anemones (*A. coronaria*), which have been developed from the wild Mediterranean windflower (see page 128), can be persuaded to flower throughout autumn, winter and spring in mild areas. To achieve a succession of blooms, corms should be planted in both autumn and spring, when, in the right conditions, flowers can follow within a few weeks of planting.

The 'De Caen' anemones have single blooms, perfect in shape, with dark centres and a wide range of hues which include deep purple blue, pale rose, white, pink and vivid scarlet. The silvery white halo at the petal bases, contrasts with the dark brooding centres, giving these flowers great character. 'Saint Brigid' anemones are from similar origins but have double flowers, less shapely but longer lasting and often more striking in their colours.

Indoor bulbs continue to bring winter cheer, even in the coldest of regions. *Hippeastrum*, a member of the *Amaryllis* family, are available in a variety of colours including pink, red, white and various shades in between. The variety 'Apple Blossom' (see right, below) is rendered even more beautiful by the dark pencilling that runs through its petals.

PRIMULA WHITEI

Among the diverse groups of primroses and their relatives, come the so-called petiolarid primulas. Although most of these are rather exacting in their growing requirements, needing cool, moist summers and cold, wet but largely frost-free winters, the early flowers are so beautiful that they are worth the trouble. The clusters of flowers, in clear mauve, purple-blue or white tones, each with a greenish centre, grow from the centres of the mealy rosettes of pale leaves. In warm regions, it is essential to shade these plants in summer, and to continue to reproduce them by collecting seed and sowing it cool.

HELLEBORUS ORIENTALIS Hybrids

The finest of the garden hellebores, oriental hellebores are the result of hybridizing *Hellebore orientalis* with other species (see page 132). They come in such gentle shades as pure white, apple blossom pink, deep purple to black and strong maroon, and many sport distinctive markings on the insides of the flowers. These may be spots, blotches or mottling, usually in deep black or purple, and are especially effective on pale or white flowers. Seedling plants of this quality would be an excellent choice to plant, not only for their own beauty, but because they can be used to throw good progeny and hence to develop a fine collection of plants.

127

HIPPEASTRUM 'Apple Blossom'

One of the most dramatic bulbs for the greenhouse or sub-tropical garden is hippeastrum. In mid- to late winter a thick, rigid stem emerges from the large bulb, reaching about 30cm (12in) before unfolding three or four huge, waxy blooms. These are pink and white, often marked with faint lines, and sweetly fragrant. To make them flower year after year, feed when in active growth with a high potash fertilizer and allow them to go dormant for the summer months, drying them off while still in pots. Begin to water in autumn, sparingly at first, ready for the next startling eruption.

HEPATICA TRANSSILVANICA

Close relatives of the anemones, hepaticas have small flowers in exquisitely clean colours, sky blue in the wild, as well as white and pink. *Hepatica nobilis* has prettily marked leaves, but *H. transsilvanica* is the showiest of the group, with biggish, lobed foliage growing straight from the ground, and azure flowers which first show in late winter and last through to early spring. Hepaticas are easy to multiply by division, best carried out when the plant is dying down to dormancy in early summer.

VIOLA 'Duchesse de Parme'

In the nineteenth century, so-called Parma violets were so fashionable that almost every keen gardener grew them, and most florists sold several different kinds. The flowers are always double, richly fragrant and usually produced on fine, long stems. They need to be grown in a protected cold frame or in a warm climate. To ensure a steady succession of big and beautiful flowers, grow them like strawberries: remove side runners and ensure that each mature plant grows in rich, fertile soil full of organic matter. Unless kept moist and healthily growing, the leaves can be ruined by red spider mite.

DAPHNE ODORA

Almost every member of the *Daphne* genus has fragrant flowers, but *D. odora* is particularly sweetly scented. The petal backs are purplish pink, but the flowers open to pearly white from late winter through to spring.

In *D. odora* 'Aureomarginata', the most widely grown cultivar, the laurel-like foliage is gold edged. Relatively hardy, but not capable of tolerating sustained frost, this bushy shrub should be planted in a sheltered spot or against a warm wall in a very cold garden. Just lime tolerant, it is happiest in neutral or acid soil which does not become too dry.

In a cool conservatory, lengthening days will coax some of the late winter tender bulbs into bloom. Besides the orange clivias and Cape cowslips (see page 124), which mostly flower in warm orange, yellows and purple-mauve, comes *Veltheimia capensis*, whose poker-shaped, dusky red blooms are reminiscent of kniphofias. Although not frost hardy, these plants tolerate surprisingly low temperatures and can therefore be used to decorate conservatories where heating is on a budget. They look especially delightful with camellia foliage to back them, parma violets (see left, centre) in the foreground and perhaps in association with freesias or homerias. Aloes, also from Africa, will tolerate relatively low temperatures, too, as long as they do not freeze and as long as they are grown in very dry conditions. One of the most handsome of these succulents, *Aloe ferox* has huge, fleshy, well-armed foliage. When it reaches about 2m (6ft), it produces a huge spike of burning orange blooms.

Outdoors, the choice of collectable flowers is growing, although plants still need to be tough to bloom this early in the year. Sweet violets, especially winter-blooming kinds like *Viola* 'Quatre Saisons', and pansies will carry flower for a long time, particularly during mild spells.

In a rock garden, the first of the saxifrages begin to show colour. One of the earliest, *Saxifraga* 'Gregor Mendel' (syn *S. apiculata*) has creamy yellow flowers held proudly above clusters of neat, green rosettes. To propagate these, simply remove rosettes and replant them in gritty, free-draining compost. Tufa, a kind of porous, spongy rock, is an ideal medium for such tiny, cushion plants. The stone should be soft enough for a planting hole to be gouged out, and a tiny pinch of compost used to wedge in the plant. Other rock plants that grow happily on tufa include such wild primulas as *P. x pubescens*, the primrose relatives, *Dionysia,* and little ferns like the maidenhair spleenwort (*Asplenium trichomanes*).

RIGHT: *The Mediterranean windflower* (Anemone coronaria) *blooms sporadically through autumn, winter and then more prolifically in spring.*

ABOVE: *Hybrids of the oriental hellebore* (Helleborus orientalis) *occur in a broad spread of pinks, purples and creamy whites. They interbreed readily and are prolific seeders.*

A variable western Mediterranean species, the semi-evergreen *Clematis cirrhosa* (see right, centre) brings the huge clematis genus into the winter months. It is equally happy in a conservatory or outdoors, provided frost is only light to moderate. Flowers, usually parchment coloured with brownish red flecks on their insides, begin to open soon after the shortest day, but the plant is at its best at winter's end, when the young, fresh green foliage has begun to emerge, contrasting with the bronzed older leaves and the massed flowers. The cultivar *C. cirrhosa* 'Freckles' is an excellent selection, having much more prominent speckling inside the flowers. These plants are best left unpruned, unless they have grown straggly, in which case the best time for a clean-up is as soon as the last flowers have begun to fade. This allows new growth time to mature and to develop flowering shoots.

Gorse (*Ulex europaeus*), a tough plant from the 'blasted heaths' of Northern Europe, seems able to bloom cheerfully in the face of the nastiest weather, even braving late winter blizzards. The double-flowered form 'Flore Pleno' is best for gardens, but courage is needed to grow this plant since it is so viciously armed. Deep blue scillas would contrast excitingly with the yellow of the gorse flowers and with the brooding dark green of its stems and prickles, but on the dry or stony ground best suited to it, onion-scented *Ipheion uniflorum* might do better. The cultivar 'Wisley Blue' has sky-coloured flowers, a more positive colour than the common wild form, but better still is the deep purple-blue 'Froyle Mill'.

Laurels may be unexciting, workaday shrubs, but the function they perform in a garden, either as sheltering plants or to create an evergreen screen, is invaluable. In a small space or where a low-growing variety is needed, *Prunus laurocerasus* 'Otto Luyken' is one of the handiest. Its long spikes of small white late winter flowers are followed by red then black cherry-like fruit.

BERGENIA CRASSIFOLIA

Also known as Saint Patrick's cabbage or pig squeak because a leaf tugged between finger and thumb squeaks, Bergenia crassifolia grows wild in the Asian steppes where winters are ruthless. Its rounded, ruffled leaves are evergreen, but the foliage of Bergenia purpurascens turns bronze or purple in winter. These plants are loveliest in late winter when the strange swollen buds at the bases of the leaves swell and burst to reveal purplish pink or white blooms. As spring approaches, the flower stems lengthen until all the blooms are held well clear of the foliage. To develop new plants, break off pieces of old stem, with or without roots, and plant these in any soil.

CLEMATIS CIRRHOSA

131

The flower buds of Clematis cirrhosa appear in late autumn, but few open before midwinter to reveal parchment-coloured sepals, many of which are flecked with rusty markings on their insides. Relatively hardy, but unable to survive in sustained frost, this plant needs the protection of a warm wall or a sheltering host plant in which to climb. If frost happens to cut it to the ground, the roots will probably produce new shoots.

PRUNUS LAUROCERASUS 'Otto Luyken'

Prunus laurocerasus 'Otto Luyken' has a fairly rigid growth habit with branches held at an acute angle, making a low shuttlecock shape. The narrow, pointed leaves make a neat background for the profusion of white flowers which appear all over the shrub in late winter and early spring, held erect like birthday candles. Although these shrubs will stay neat without any attention being paid to them, they are amenable to being clipped once a year to develop them into low, informal hedging.

Few winter plants have such distinctive characters,

such subtle coloration or attract so strongly,

but with such modest beauty

Hellebores

Welcome though they are, during the darkest months, many winter-flowering species are noticeable because of their season rather than for their especial beauty, but the hellebore would stand out at any time. The clean symmetry of the flower, with its central stamens and five radiating petal-like sepals, is arresting. The colours, even on those varieties with suffusions of steely grey-green, metallic black or brooding purple are pleasing, making the plants stand out in the border, but never prominently enough to jar or clash with their sombre winter setting.

Few flowers, except perhaps euphorbias, can outdo the hellebores for longevity. On some species, the first blooms emerge in late autumn and continue to carry remnants of beauty well into spring, when their colour has declined to a more leafy green, and the seed capsules have ripened and burst. In many species the foliage, too, is handsome. The Lenten rose (*Helleborus foetidus*), for instance, has distinctive, palmate evergreen leaves which give the plants an architectural standing even before the first green, maroon-edged blooms open.

Among special treasures, the Christmas rose (*H. niger*) has the whitest flowers (see page 116). Such named forms as 'Potters Wheel' are better than unselected seedlings. The so-called oriental hybrids exhibit the most interesting range of flower colours and shapes (see page 127). These have been raised from a number of species, mainly the white or red *H. orientalis* with admixtures from the yellowish green-flowered *H. odorus*, the deep brooding purple-black *H. atrorubens* and the bi-coloured blackish and green *H. torquatus*.

Most hellebores are evergreen, but exceptions include one of the commoner species *H. viridis*, whose foliage dies back each summer. Most are happy on any cool, moist soil in partial shade. They are not difficult to grow, but some species take a while to establish themselves.

FROM THE TOP:

A European woodland perennial, Helleborus viridis *has been naturalized in some of the woods of New England.*

Helleborus *'Pluto', a rare dark-flowered oriental hybrid, inherited its two-tone flowers, from one of its parents,* H. torquatus.

The hybrid Helleborus *'Dawn' boasts the largest flowers, sometimes reaching more than 9cm (3½in) across.*

RIGHT: Helleborus *'Party Dress' hybrids have a more ruffled or fuller effect than most hellebores, due to the fact that some of the nectaries have become sepal-like or petal-like in form.*

ANEMONE BLANDA 'White Splendour'

In the wild, *Anemone blanda* has pretty blue flowers with rayed petals giving an almost daisy-like appearance. Garden forms come in a wider choice of colours ranging from the brilliant cerise of *A. blanda* 'Radar' through pale lilac to near white. 'White Splendour' is easily the finest form in cultivation, with showy blooms, sometimes reaching up to 5cm (2in) across, in late winter to early spring. The plant is seed sterile so to bulk up stocks, lift the corms just as the last of the foliage is dying back, and cut them carefully into smaller pieces using a sharp knife. Dust the wounds with flowers of sulphur to reduce the risk of rotting and replant immediately, at least 5cm (2in) deep.

TULIPA 'Purissima'

For sheer grandeur so early in the growing season, the fosteriana or 'Emperor' tulips are unsurpassable. *Tulipa* 'Purissima' (syn. *T.* 'White Emperor') often develops buds well before the spring equinox, needing but a glimpse of sunshine for these to swell and turn greenish cream before opening to display darker centres. As they mature, the petals expand until they are more than 8cm (3in) long, increasing in brilliance and purity of colour until they are milk white, just before they fall. Tulips grow best in deep, fertile soil that is well drained but does not dry too much. Plant bulbs in autumn at least 15cm (6in) deep. Left undisturbed, they will produce increasing numbers of blooms each year, but these will decrease in size over the years.

LONICERA FRAGRANTISSIMA

Winter-blooming honeysuckles may not be a knockout for colour and spectacle, but the power of the fragrance that each of the small white blooms packs is more than enough compensation. These are large, somewhat ungainly shrubs with bland green foliage in summer and an amorphous winter outline. As the leaves fall, usually very late in autumn, pairs of flowers emerge along the stems, opening whenever there is mild weather.

At winter's end, mimosa can create a sense of optimism when used for sweetening bouquets of spring flowers with its fragrance and cheering them with its bright yellow, fluffy blooms. The evergreen mimosa genus, called more correctly *Acacia*, is vast, with representatives as diverse as fever trees and thorn scrub in the plains and hills of Africa to the quaint sensitive plant (*A. pudica*) (see page 74) which grows wild all over the tropics and wilts instantly whenever it is touched. The finest mimosas for conservatory or garden use in mild areas, are those with compact growth habits and blooms that are concentrated on the stem. Fragrance, too, is essential and of those which are the most deeply fragrant, the easiest to grow is common wattle (*A. dealbata*). A more attractive species, however, is *A. baileyana* (see page 137).

The last days of winter can provide some of the finest indoor shows of the year, especially when blooms of azaleas, cyclamen and primulas move to their final climax. These can be joined by the last of the spring bulbs (tulips, hyacinths and narcissus) to have been forced under glass for early blooming. As these pass their peak, plants that flower on increasing day length will begin to come into flower, joined by foliage plants whose growth begins to accelerate now in response to increased day length and light intensity regardless of how cold it may be on the other side of the glass.

There is a down side, of course, in that greenhouse and conservatory pests are also beginning to wake up. Whitefly and red spider mite can begin to be troublesome this early, especially during bright, sunny spells when midday temperatures under glass are surprisingly high. Now is the perfect time to gain control over the worst of these pests, before their populations reach epidemic proportions. Smokes and fumigants can work well here, to be followed later either by a pesticide regime or biological predators. In an all-organic garden, a reasonable level of control is possible by including the right plants in the display, tobacco or tagetes to deter whitefly, for instance, or by using sticky traps and ensuring scrupulous hygiene.

Outdoors, you may be itching to get to work on borders where over-wintered weeds are beginning to grow and new seedlings are popping up, but avoid the temptation of walking on beds or borders where the soil is still cold and wet. Moist soils, especially heavy ones with a high clay content, are all too easily compacted, driving out the air and spoiling the crumbly structure. Once damaged in this way soils can be difficult to restore to their fertile best. A short cut to good soil structure is to keep dressing the surface and incorporating well-rotted organic material.

Time is running out, too, for completing the last of those winter jobs that you may have been contemplating for the past few months. Shrubs that bloom after the longest day, buddlejas or tree mallows, for example, should be pruned hard back to promote strong, new flowering shoots. The last of the climbing roses should have been pruned and tied in by now and any remaining herbaceous plants trimmed of their dead stems and given a light feed to help them into growth. As you work, you could be surprised and delighted by unlooked for flowers: a sweet pall of fragrance might draw your attention to previously unnoticed greenish flowers of evergreen *Daphne laureola*, which are identical in shape to the more conspicuous purplish blooms of deciduous *Daphne mezereum*. In shade, *Trachystemon orientalis*, a coarse-leaved ground cover, has a brief spell of beauty when its soft blue-and-white, sweptback blooms open on short sprays, displaying pointed stigma and stamens for a week or two

Nothing is so pure and beautiful
as the wild primrose
(Primula vulgaris).

135

before the large foliage expands and fulfils its function as a weed-suppressor.

Primroses begin to open in earnest, not only the traditional wild yellow kinds, but garden forms of *Primula juliana* with lilac, pink or brick-red blooms. One of the most dependable is *P. juliana* 'Wanda', whose yellow-eyed, deep magenta blooms are produced in such profusion that the foliage all but disappears. Incapable of seeding itself, *P. juliana* 'Wanda' often pollinates other primroses to produce strange children with dark foliage and interesting flower colours. Primroses are fecund plants and if you can collect seed or preserve self-sown seedlings you could be delighted at the diversity of the offspring.

ABOVE: *The flowers of the common pasque flower* (Pulsatilla vulgaris) *appear at the very end of winter, their buds protected from frost by a furry covering.*

In regions where cold weather prevents frost tender mimosa from flowering outdoors, colour comes from other sources. The small yellow flowers of the cornelian cherry (*Cornus mas*) are in full bloom by now. Nearer to the ground, in dappled shade, the extraordinary *Hacquetia epipactis* (see right, centre) sports little golden tufts surrounded by a collar of lime green. Sweet violets, whether wild *Viola odorata* or its cultivars like *V.* 'Amiral Avellon' or the leather-scented, pink *V.* 'Coeur d'Alsace', can be encouraged to spread their runners among primroses, closing the connecting link between winter and spring. Not only are their flowers sweetly scented but their foliage is, too, making a walk through the woodland garden a delight even after the last of the flowers are over.

Primroses and violets like to flower in full sun, but prefer to be shaded from its full strength in summer, making them ideal subjects, along with narcissus, bluebells and wood anemones, for growing under deciduous trees. Most of their annual life-cycle is completed before the trees come into full foliage, but often in gardens such beneficent shade is not always available. In a border, however, siting shade-loving spring flowers between taller perennials will go a long way towards achieving similar conditions.

In full sun, Mediterranean bulbs, or rather bulbs which enjoy Mediterranean conditions, emerge and flower with surprising speed. Besides wild grape hyacinths, small tulip species and scillas there are plants with more sophisticated blooms. The curious flowers of *Hermodactylus tuberosus* (see right, below) make intriguing companions to vivid red anemones. The pale green petals of this iris relative look as though they are tipped with black satin. Plenty of hot, baking sun is essential to ripen the tubers and produce flowers. Once established, the root stock will creep over a surprisingly large area, first throwing up leaves in midwinter then following these up with late winter or early spring blooms.

ACACIA BAILEYANA

Also known as the Cootamundra wattle, *Acacia baileyana* is more showy, with graceful arching branches, than some other mimosa trees. The small golden yellow 'mimosa balls' are more concentrated on the stem and the ferny, blue-grey foliage is slightly more durable than in the more fragrant *A. dealbata*. The latter has the disadvantage of a lax habit and a tendency to drop foliage during summer on plants grown below its branches. Outdoors, this creates few problems as the leaves simply blow away and rot, but in a conservatory it can create an untidy mess.

HACQUETIA EPIPACTIS

Moist shade or semi-shade suits this intriguing little plant best. The lime-green-and-golden colour scheme of the flowers suggest euphorbia, but *Hacquetia epipactis* belongs to the same family as carrots, parsley and Queen Anne's lace. After flowering, the rounded leaves grow up over the developing seed capsules, but seldom reach more than about 15cm (6in) in height. It makes a charming companion to deep blue scillas or

chionodoxas and to every species of violet. In moist, shaded soil it will seed around freely, but never becomes a nuisance. It can also be divided and replanted in late spring.

HERMODACTYLUS TUBEROSUS

The exotic-looking widow or snakeshead iris comes from southern Europe. Its sweetly fragrant blooms are yellowish green with large dark brown, almost black tips to the petals. The flowers last as long when cut and placed in a vase as they do growing naturally outdoors, making them valuable plants in late winter. This lime-loving species is fully hardy, requiring hot sun in summer to ripen the finger-like tubers. Propagate by division in late summer.

137

Crocuses are among the brightest of the flowers to mark the turning point of the year

Crocus

BELOW: *Beige when closed, with dark purple feathering,* Crocus corsicus *opens to reveal bright violet-purple inner petals.*

CENTRE: *Large Dutch crocuses come in blue, purple or white shades. Many, such as* Crocus *'Pickwick', have feathered or striped blooms.*

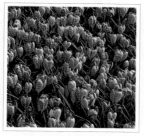

ABOVE: Crocus chrysanthus *'Zwanenberg Bronze' has feathered bronze striping on its petal backs and brilliant orange inner petals.*

No flower responds so quickly to a change in the weather than crocuses, and the briefest burst of sunshine makes them open their petals wide to tempt an early bee hunting for nectar. Moreover, with careful selection, it is possible furnish a garden with crocus blooms from midwinter until the beginning of spring, as well as with a small number of choice autumn-flowering species.

The most commonly grown garden crocuses have been developed over several centuries by the Dutch from the wild species *Crocus vernus*. These are good pot subjects if grown cool and brought into flower, indoors, several months before their natural flowering time outside.

The most popular species is the southern European *C. chrysanthus*. In the wild this is yellow, but it has been hybridized to produce such glorious cultivars as 'Zwanenburg Bronze', 'Snow Bunting', cream, and the purple-and-white *C.* 'Sultan'. These are all much smaller than the Dutch hybrids.

For naturalizing in grassland, *C. tommasinianus* bulks up so fast in reasonable soil that it wins on sheer quantity. Spreading from both seed and underground runners, this is a crocus to colonize in a meadow garden where it will precede daffodils and other spring plants, opening its greyish-backed flowers in sunlight to decorate the turf with a million lilac stars.

Among the loveliest colour combinations are two very closely related species, *C. imperati* and *C. corsicus*. These have beige outer petals, richly striped in dark brown. When the sun coaxes each bloom to open, the inner flower is bright lilac blue with glowing orange stigma and gold stamens.

Most crocuses prefer full sun, but will thrive in soil that is neither rich in organic material nor especially fertile. If you feed them at all, restrict your fertilizing to applying a high potash plant food in spring, before the plants set seed. In grass, never mow until the flowers have had time to set seed.

LEFT: *Two contrasting tones of purple blue and white make a distinctive display in* Crocus chrysanthus *'Ladykiller', especially in sun when the flower opens wide.*

Seasonal plant index

The plants recommended in this book are arranged alphabetically according to the season they normally flower in. Latin names only have been used here. Common names can be found in the general index (see page 143).

Spring

Winter

General index

This general index lists plants by their common names. The seasonal plant index (see pages 140-142) lists all recommended plants seasonally according to their Latin names. Page numbers in italic refer to illustrations.

144

Acknowledgments

The publisher thanks the photographers and organisations for their kind permission to reproduce the following photographs in this book:

1 Marijke Heuff; 2-3 Marcus Harpur; 4-5 S&O Mathews; 6-7 Jerry Harpur; 8-11 S&O Mathews; 12 Charles Mann; 13 left S&O Mathews; 13 right Andrew Lawson; 14 Marijke Heuff; 15 left S&O Mathews; 15 right Linda Burgess; 16 Andrew Lawson; 17 above Clive Nichols /Beth Chatto; 17 centre S&O Mathews; 18 above Neil Campbell-Sharp; 18 centre John Glover; 19-20 Andrew Lawson; 21 above Marijke Heuff; 21 centre Andrew Lawson; 21 below Clive Nichols; 22 above John Glover; 22 centre Anne Hyde; 22 below John Glover; 22-23 Andrew Lawson; 24 Eric Crichton; 25 centre S&O Mathews; 25 below S&O Mathews; 26 above S&O Mathews; 26 centre Andrew Lawson; 26 below S&O Mathews; 28 Andrew Lawson; 29 above and centre Andrew Lawson; 29 below Jerry Harpur; 30 above S&O Mathews; 30 centre Photos Horticultural; 31 Andrew Lawson; 33 above John Glover; 33 centre Jerry Harpur; 33 below Andrew Lawson; 34 S&O Mathews; 35 above S&O Mathews; 35 centre Charles Mann; 36-37 S&O Mathews; 37 above and below Anne Hyde; 37 centre S & O Mathews; 38 below Andrew Lawson; 39 above S&O Mathews; 39 centre Jacqui Hurst; 40 S&O Mathews; 41 above Andrew Lawson; 41 centre Marijke Heuff; 41 below S&O Mathews; 42 above Photos Horticultural; 42 centre Andrew Lawson; 43 Jacqui Hurst; 44 Marijke Heuff (Seitje Stuurman); 45 John Glover; 46 Linda Burgess; 47 left Linda Burgess; 47 right Marijke Heuff (Ton ter Linden); 48 above Derek Gould; 48 centre Clive Nichols; 48 below S&O Mathews; 49 S&O Mathews; 50-51 Neil Campbell-Sharp (Mottisfont Rose Garden); 51 above Clive Nichols; 51 centre Jerry Harpur; 51 below John Glover; 52 above Photos Horticultural; 52 centre Andrew Lawson; 53 S&O Mathews; 54 Marijke Heuff; 55 above and centre Andrew Lawson; 55 below Clive Nichols; 56 above John Glover; 56 below Marijke Heuff; 57 Jacqui Hurst; 58 Charles Mann; 59 above Charles Mann; 59 centre Photos Horticultural; 59 below Marijke Heuff; 60 above Andrew Lawson; 60 centre Neil Campbell-Sharp; 61 Andrew Lawson; 62 above Andrew Lawson; 62 centre and below Clive Nichols; 62-63 Andrew Lawson; 64 Anne Hyde; 65 above Clive Nichols; 65 centre Anne Hyde; 66 above Clive Nichols; 66 centre Andrew Lawson; 66 below S&O Mathews; 68 above Clive Nichols; 68 centre Andrew Lawson; 68 below Clive Nichols; 69 Clive Nichols; 70 John Glover; 71 above Anne Hyde; 71 centre A-Z Botanical; 71 below S&O Mathews; 72 Insight London /Jack Townsend; 73 above S&O Mathews; 73 centre and below Clive Nichols; 74 above Marijke Heuff; 74 centre Photos Horticultural; 76 Magnum /Ernst Haas; 77 left Neil Campbell-Sharp; 77 right Anne Hyde; 78 S&O Mathews; 79 left Clive Nichols; 79 right Andrew Lawson; 80 above Andrew Lawson; 80 centre Garden Picture Library /J S Sira; 80 below Marijke Heuff; 81 Clive Nichols; 82 Anne Hyde; 83 above John Glover; 83 centre Eric Crichton; 84 above Jerry Harpur; 84 centre S&O Mathews; 84 below A-Z Botanical /Anthony Seinet; 85 S&O Mathews; 86 Eric Crichton; 87 above Neil Campbell-Sharp; 87 centre Jerry Harpur; 88 above and below S&O Mathews; 88 centre Insight London /Jack Townsend; 89 Garden Picture Library /Sunniva Harte; 91 above Garden Picture Library /John Glover; 91 centre S&O Mathews; 91 below Eric Crichton; 92 above A-Z Botanical /Malkolm Warrington; 92 centre Jacqui Hurst; 92 below John Fielding Slide Library; 92-93 S&O Mathews; 94 above Brigitte Perdereau; 94 centre Andrew Lawson; 94 below S&O Mathews; 95 S&O Mathews; 96 Clive Nichols; 97 above Andrew Lawson; 97 below Clive Nichols; 98-99 Michèle Lamontagne; 99 above John Glover; 99 centre Michèle Lamontagne; 99 below S&O Mathews; 100 John Glover; 101 centre Andrew Lawson; 101 below S&O Mathews; 102 centre Andrew Lawson; 102 below S&O Mathews; 103 Clive Nichols; 104 above Harry Smith Collection; 104 centre Clive Nichols; 104 below A-Z Botanical /Mike Danson; 104-105 Harry Smith Collection; 106 S&O Mathews; 107 above and below S&O Mathews; 107 centre Andrew Lawson; 108 John Glover; 109 left Derek Gould; 109 right A-Z Botanical /Mike Dauson; 110 Harry Smith Collection; 111 left Andrew Lawson; 111 right Andrew Lawson; 112 above and centre S&O Mathews; 113 John Glover; 114 Derek Gould; 115 above Clive Nichols; 115 centre S&O Mathews; 115 below A-Z Botanical; 116 Andrew Lawson; 117 Clive Nichols; 118 Derek Gould; 119 above Clive Nichols; 119 centre Michèle Lamontagne ; 120 above Marcus Harpur; 120 centre and below Andrew Lawson; 120-121 Andrew Lawson /Painswick Rococo Garden; 122 Andrew Lawson; 123 above Eric Crichton; 123 below S&O Mathews; 124 above Andrew Lawson; 124 centre S&O Mathews; 125 Andrew Lawson; 127 above Harry Smith Collection; 127 centre Clive Nichols; 127 below A-Z Botanical /Marion Bull; 128 above Andrew Lawson; 128 centre John Glover; 129 Garden Picture Library /John Glover; 130 Andrew Lawson; 131 centre Clive Nichols; 131 below Jerry Harpur; 132 Andrew Lawson; 132-133 Andrew Lawson; 134 above and centre Garden Picture Library /Chris Burrows; 134 below Clive Nichols; 136 S&O Mathews; 137 above Garden Picture Library /Howard Rice; 137 centre Andrew Lawson; 137 below S&O Mathews; 138-139 Garden Picture Library /Chris Burrows; 139 above Andrew Lawson; 139 centre John Glover; 139 below Michèle Lamontagne.